Mathematical activities

MATHEMATICAL ACTIVITIES

A resource book for teachers

Brian Bolt

CAMBRIDGE UNIVERSITY PRESS
Cambridge, New York, Melbourne, Madrid, Cape Town, Singapore, São Paulo

Cambridge University Press
The Edinburgh Building, Cambridge CB2 8RU, UK

Published in the United States of America by Cambridge University Press, New York

www.cambridge.org
Information on this title: www.cambridge.org/9780521285186

First published 1982
Seventeenth printing 2000
Re-issued in this digitally printed version 2007

A catalogue record for this publication is available from the British Library

ISBN 978-0-521-28518-6 paperback

For the purposes of this digital reprinting the commentary
section has been reproduced in black and white text

ACKNOWLEDGEMENTS
The author and the publisher would like to thank the following
for permission to reproduce copyright material.
Collection Haags Gemeentemuseum, The Hague: M. C. Escher,
Swans and Horseman (page 29), © SPADEM, Paris 1981 /
Beeldrecht, Amsterdam
National Railway Museum, York: Weatherhill Engine (page 38)
Mansell Collection: Albrecht Dürer, *Melancholia* (page 118)

Contents

Page numbers in *italics* refer to the commentary.

Preface

With the present pattern of schools and the current vogue
for mixed ability teaching there is a very real danger that
the children with an aptitude for mathematics will rarely
have their appetite for the subject whetted. It is my own
opinion and that of many of my colleagues that our own
interest in mathematics grew from the stimulation we
received from teachers and books at an early age – long
before decisions about examinations were taken. This interest was generated not only by the formal mathematics
lessons but often by ideas which come from unusual puzzles
or games, or patterns which a teacher introduced or were
seen in some publication.

An interest in mathematical puzzles is widespread; it
generates creative thinking and motivates individuals in a
way that a standard text book exercise can rarely achieve.
Unfortunately many teachers do not have the background
to provide these activities so their children fail to have the
appropriate stimulus at a critical period in their education.
Such considerations eventually persuaded me to run a weekly
maths club on Saturday mornings for interested 9–12 year
olds. I stressed the word 'interested' rather than 'gifted'
and the enthusiasm with which this club was received by the
children far exceeded my expectations. With thirty or more
eager children turning up each week I have been highly moti-
vated to find suitable activities to stimulate them.

This book contains some of the ideas I have used in the
five years of this club and the many years I ran a similar
club at Exeter School for an older age group. I have written
them up with middle school children particularly in mind
but experience has shown many of the activities could
be used with mathematically able children of other ages.
If the activity has not been met before then it is usually
found of interest regardless of the age of the participant.

Brian Bolt
School of Education
University of Exeter

Introduction

The activities in this book have been chosen to stimulate
and encourage the reader to develop his appreciation of
number, spatial concepts and mathematical thinking. This
has been achieved with a mixture of investigations, puzzles
and games. Where appropriate an activity has a solution or
commentary at the end of the book but it is hoped that
the reader will only turn to this section after attempting
the activity for himself.

The book is not meant to be read in any specific order
as each activity is independent of the others, unless stated.
It is essentially a source book of ideas which, on the whole,
would not normally be met with in the school curriculum.

A calculator is required for some of the investigations
where, with one exception, it is used as a tool to take the
drudgery from the arithmetic and allow the reader to discover some number properties which would otherwise be
inaccessible.

The games usually involve two people and some other
activities gain by having more than one person involved
because of the different insights they can bring to bear
on a particular problem.

Materials

Practical work is envisaged and should be encouraged in
many of the spatial activities. Looking at a drawing can
never replace handling a model or moving a linkage. Nothing
elaborate is required however, just the usual card, scissors,
compass, ruler, glue, drawing board and a pinboard.

ACTIVITIES

1 Three in a line

Get some squared paper and some counters.

The object of this activity is to put as many counters onto a squared board as you can so that

  (i)   no more than one counter is put on a square,
  (ii) no three counters are in a straight line.

Diagrams (a), (b) and (c) each show a 3 x 3 board where two counters have already been placed on the board. Show how to add four more counters to each board so that no three counters are in line.

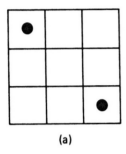

(a)

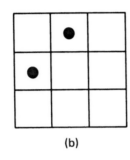

(b)

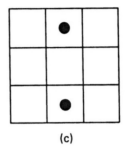

(c)

On a 4 x 4 board it is possible to place eight counters using the same rule that no three lie on a line. One person started by putting four counters in the centre as shown in (d). A second put four counters in the corners as in (e) while a third started as in (f).

How many counters can you add to these boards before getting three in a line?

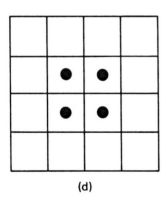

(d)

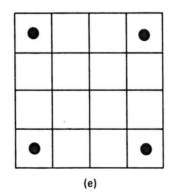

(e)

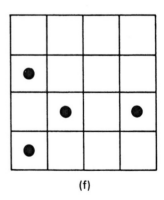

(f)

Try to do better by starting yourself.

When you have found a way of putting eight counters on a 4 x 4 board, try putting ten counters on a 5 x 5 board.

2 Pawns on a chessboard

This is the classical problem of placing sixteen pawns on a chessboard so that no three of the pawns are in line.

It is essentially the same situation as in the previous activity, but with an 8 × 8 board it is not so easy to spot when three pawns are in line.

The diagram shows several lines of pawns which are not at all obvious at first sight namely *ABC*, *ECD* and *FCG*.

When you think you have correctly placed sixteen pawns on an 8 × 8 board so that no three are in a line, get someone else to check your solution before looking at the solution at the back of this book.

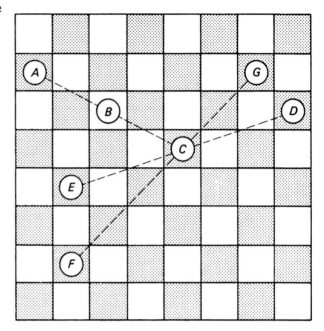

3 Avoid three

This game can be played with pawns or draughts on a chessboard, counters on squared paper, or pegs on a pegboard.

Players take turns to add a piece to the board. A player loses the game when he plays a piece to make a line of three.

Note the game could never exceed seventeen moves because the largest number of pieces which can be placed on an 8 × 8 board without having three in line is sixteen. The skill in the game is to select patterns of play which force your opponent into having to complete a line.

In the diagram there are only twelve pieces on the board but they are so placed that the next person to play will have to make a line of three and thus lose. Check each empty square in turn to convince yourself that this is so. A straight-edge may help.

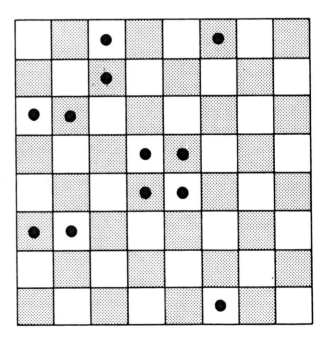

4 Curves of pursuit

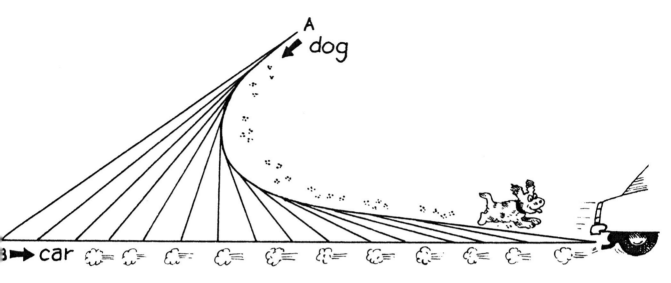

You must have seen, at some time, a dog chase a car or a cyclist. Have you ever considered the path it takes? The dog does not think ahead and run to where the car will be, but usually runs towards the position of the car at that instant.

The drawing above shows the path of a dog which starts running towards a car which it first notices at B. The car is travelling at a constant speed along the line BC and it is assumed that the dog can run at half the speed of the car.

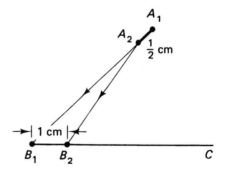

The path can be easily constructed in the following way.

Draw a line B_1C to represent the path of the car. Then take a point A_1 (anywhere will do) to represent the dog's starting position.

Draw a line from A_1 to B_1. This is the direction in which the dog starts to run. Because a dog cannot easily change direction between strides it will run in this direction for a short distance to A_2. This is represented in the drawing by $\frac{1}{2}$ cm.

But while the dog is running from A_1 to A_2 the car has travelled from B_1 to B_2, a distance of 1 cm in the drawing.

At A_2 the dog changes direction towards the car at B_2 and takes a stride in this direction while the car travels to B_3. The process is repeated until the dog's path is found.

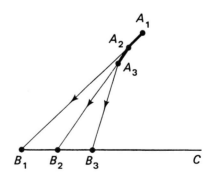

Try first to make a drawing more or less like the one shown here. Then experiment with what happens if, for example, the car travels on a circle, or the relative speeds of the dog and car change. The possibilities are endless!

5 The misguided missiles

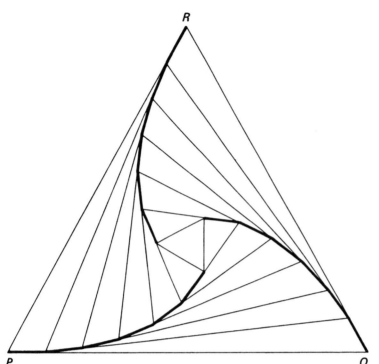

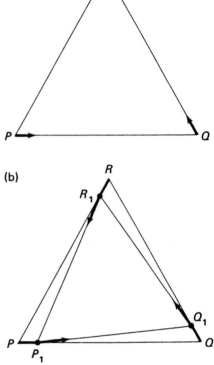

This interesting drawing is another example of finding curves of pursuit. In this case imagine three guided missiles P, Q and R based at three points each 100 km apart at the vertices of an equilateral triangle. The three missiles are all launched at the same time. P homes onto Q, Q homes onto R, and R homes onto P. At regular intervals the missiles change direction to home onto the new position of their targets. The sequence of diagrams (a) to (d) shows how to construct the path of each missile as it chases its neighbour.

Start by drawing an equilateral triangle whose sides are all 10 cm. Mark the points P_1, Q_1, R_1, 1 cm from the points P, Q, R, and draw the triangle $P_1 Q_1 R_1$. Now mark the points P_2, Q_2, R_2, 1 cm from P_1, Q_1, R_1, and draw $P_2 Q_2 R_2$. Continue this process, always marking off along the sides of the last triangle formed, until the missiles explode in the centre!

What would the paths look like if you started with four missiles at the corners of a square?

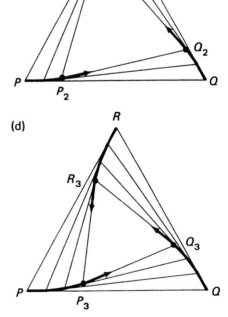

6 Pattern

Mathematics is all about the analysis and use of pattern. These may be number patterns or geometric patterns. The attractive design here has been formed by fitting together four of the drawings from the previous activity concerned with the pursuit curves of guided missiles. Many other attractive designs can result from the same starting point. All that is required is some patience and careful drawings.

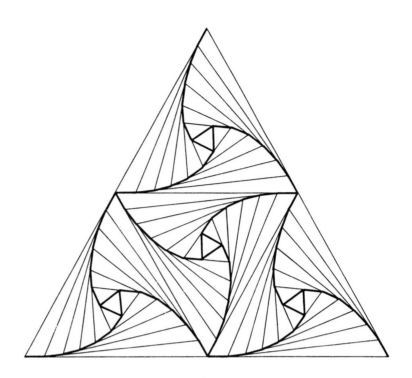

7 Two halves make a whole

Show how to cut the shaded shape A into two pieces which can be rearranged to make any of the shapes $B, C, D, E, F,$ and G.

5

8 Make your own dice

Each of the three shapes shown can be folded up to make a
dice. In each case three of the numbers are missing. Show
how to number the squares correctly so that the number on
the opposite faces of the cube add up to 7.

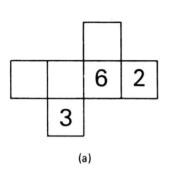

(a)

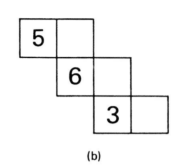

(b)

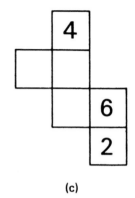

(c)

9 Matchstick triangles

Arrange nine matches to
form four small equilateral
triangles as shown. Now
find a way of arranging only
six of the matches to form
four triangles of the same
shape and size.

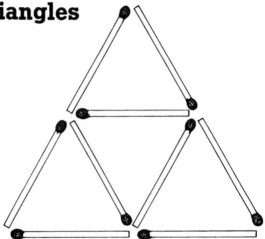

10 The farmer's sheep-pens

This drawing shows how a
farmer used thirteen hurdles
to make six identical sheep
pens. Unfortunately one of
the hurdles was damaged.

   Use twelve matchsticks to
represent the undamaged
hurdles and show how the
farmer can still make six
identical pens.

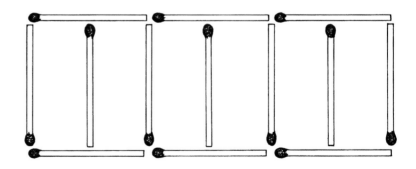

11 Map folding

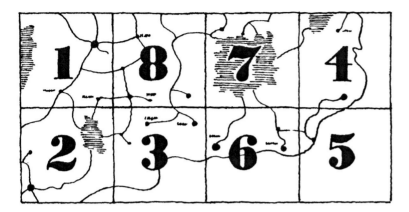

A map is twice as long as it is wide. It can be folded up into
a square, one-eighth the size of the original map, in many ways.
Number the squares as shown on a piece of paper and see
how many ways you can fold it. You can record each way by
noting down the order in which the numbers come next to
each other in the folded map.

The real test of your skill is to fold the map so that the
numbers come in the order 1, 2, 3, 4, 5, 6, 7, 8.

Now make your own puzzle by finding an unusual way to
fold a map and then numbering the squares.

12 A tricky river crossing

This is a very old puzzle. It tells of a showman travelling the
countryside on tour with a wolf, a goat, and a cabbage. He
comes to a river bank and the only means of getting across is
a small boat which can hold him with only one of the wolf,
the goat or the cabbage.

Unfortunately he dare not leave the wolf alone with the
goat or the goat alone with the cabbage for the wolf would eat
the goat and the goat would eat the cabbage. After some
thought the showman realised that he could use the boat to
transport himself and all his belongings safely across the river.
How did he do it?

13 Stretching a circle

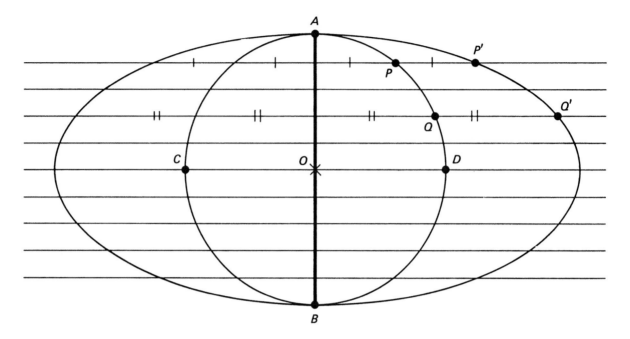

Draw a circle with radius 5 cm in the centre of a piece of
paper and mark in a diameter AOB as shown.

Next draw in the diameter COD at right-angles to AB and
extend it across the page.

Now draw a set of lines across the page parallel to CD and
about 1 cm apart.

The circle can now be stretched to double its length in the
direction of the parallel lines by marking off points such as P'
and Q' whose distance from AB is twice that of P and Q from
AB.

The new shape formed by drawing a smooth curve through
the points P', Q', etc. is called an *ellipse*.

The perimeter of this ellipse is $1\frac{1}{2}$ times the circumference
of the original circle. Test this fact using a piece of string.

How large is the area inside the ellipse compared to that
of the circle?

Draw yourself an ellipse which is formed by stretching a
circle by three times in the direction of the parallel lines.
What can you say about (i) its perimeter, (ii) its area?

Investigate the shape you would get by shrinking the circle
by half in the direction of the parallel lines.

14 The ellipse

You may have wondered when you last saw an ellipse. The fact is that whenever you look at a circle from an angle you see an ellipse. This knowledge is well appreciated by experienced artists although you will all have seen drawings by younger children where a circular object is drawn as a circle no matter from which direction it is seen.

The arches of many older stone bridges were designed to be elliptic.

The path taken by a satellite around the earth or by the earth around the sun is also an ellipse.

When you cut through a circular tree trunk at an angle the cross-section is also an ellipse.

Try cutting through a piece of cylindrical dowel or a cardboard tube or a roll of modelling clay at an angle.

Investigate the bridges in your locality and make a sketch of those with elliptic arches.

Brunel designed a railway bridge across the River Tamar at Saltash where the deck of the bridge is suspended from two massive elliptic cylinders – this is well worth a visit if you are ever in the vicinity.

15 Paper-folding an ellipse

On a piece of plain paper draw a large circle, say 16 cm in diameter. Cut the circle out carefully and on it mark a point A as shown, say 2 cm from the edge. The actual lengths are not critical but these suggested lengths give a good result. In practice you could draw around any convenient circular object such as a tin or saucer and choose any point inside the circle. Now fold the circle along any line such as PQ which makes the circle just touch the point A. Draw in the fold line after unfolding the circle. Keep repeating this process of folding and marking in the fold lines. Before long you will see an ellipse appearing surrounded by all the fold lines.

The lines are said to be *tangents* to the ellipse and form an *envelope* for it – see the diagram below.

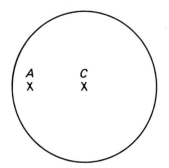

Investigate the result of taking A nearer the centre of the circle. What happens if A coincides with the centre?

Notice the way in which A and the centre of the circle C are symmetrically placed for the ellipse. They are called the *foci* of the ellipse.

When a satellite orbits the earth it does so in an elliptical path with the earth at a focus, that is a point such as A or C, and not with the earth at the centre of the ellipse.

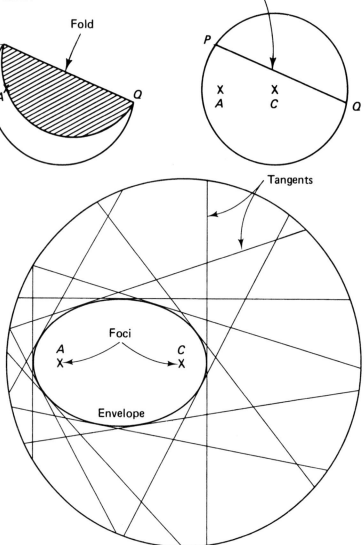

16 An ellipse using string and drawing pins

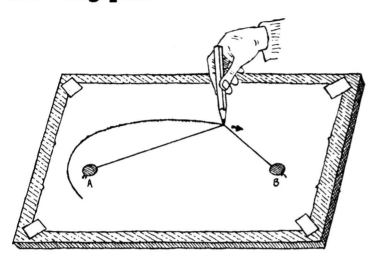

Fasten a piece of paper to a drawing board and then put two drawing pins A and B into the board, say 10 cm apart. Now take a piece of string or strong thread and tie one end to A. Next tie the other end to B so that the length of string between A and B is about 14 cm.

Using a pencil pull the string taut and, keeping it taut, move the pencil to draw in an ellipse.

Investigate the effect of using different lengths of string.

The points A and B are the foci of all the ellipses you can draw in this way.

For any one of your ellipses, what can you say about the length $AP + BP$ no matter where P is on the perimeter of the ellipse?

If Q is a point inside an ellipse what can you say about $AQ + BQ$?

17 The sliding ladder

What is the path traced out by P as the ladder AB slides down the wall? Turn the page to find out.

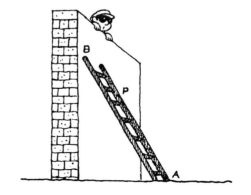

You could of course take a ladder and experiment with it, but a better approach is to take a strip of card (or geostrip) and mark points on it to represent the ends of the ladder and the point *P*. Now draw two lines *OX* and *OY* on paper to represent the ground and the wall. It now only remains to move the 'card ladder' so that *A* and *B* stay on the lines *OX* and *OY* and you trace out the path followed by *P* with a pencil.

You should recognise the path which results.

The approach to this problem can be extended in the following way and leads to some interesting results.

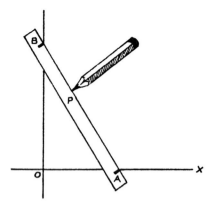

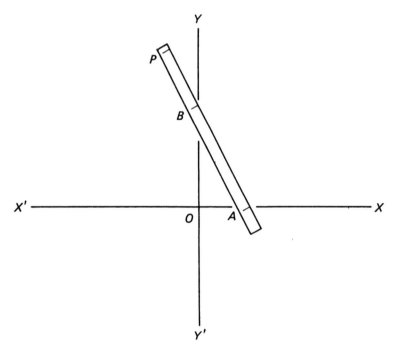

Take a strip of card (or geostrip) and mark two points *A* and *B* as shown. Let *P* be a point outside *AB*. Draw two lines *X'OX* and *Y'OY* and find the path of *P* as the card moves so that *A* always remains on *X'OX* and *B* always remains on *Y'OY*. Unlike the ladder, *A* can move onto *OX'* and *B* onto *OY'* so that a symmetrical path results.

Experiment with different positions for *A*, *B* and *P* and also with different angles between the lines *X'OX* and *Y'OY*.

But why keep to lines? How about replacing *Y'OY* by a circle?

18 The growing network

This is a game for two players sometimes known as 'Sprouts'. All that is required is a piece of paper and a pencil. Mark three points anywhere on the paper, as in (a).

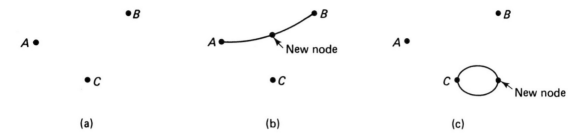

(a) (b) (c)

These points will become nodes of a network as the game progresses. The first player joins any two points by an arc and then makes a new point (node) in the middle of this arc, as in (b). Alternatively the player may draw an arc which starts and ends at the same point, but again he must add a new node in the middle of the arc, as in (c).

The next player then adds a new arc to the network and a new node in the middle of his arc. He may join his arc to any node(s) as long as the node(s) he uses do not end up with more than three branches.

As soon as a node has three branches it is 'out of bounds' and can be circled to indicate this.

The drawings in (d) show just some of the possible moves for the second player if the first player joined A to B.

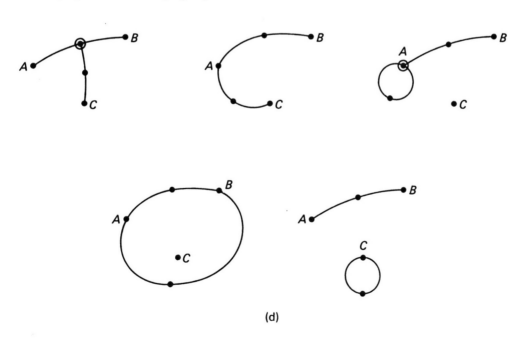

(d)

The object of the game is to prevent your opponent from being able to make a move. The last player to draw in a legitimate arc wins. One further rule: arcs may not cross over other arcs.

It pays to remember this rule, for nodes may get cut off and become unusable even though they do not have three branches.

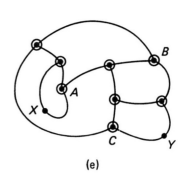

(e)

Diagram (e) shows the network produced by one game. Although at this stage there are two nodes, X and Y, which do not have three branches, they cannot be joined.

Play this game with your friends and then try the following.

(i) Try to explain why the game must end after a limited number of moves. (How many?)
(ii) Try starting with four or five points.
(iii) Investigate the effect of having 4–nodes (i.e. nodes which have *four* branches) instead of 3–nodes.

19 Cubism

Some corners are cut out of four wooden cubes.

Afterwards only two of the solids formed are the same shape.

Which two are they?

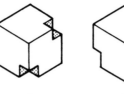      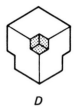

A   B   C   D

20 Matchstick squares

Remove three matches from the fifteen in the arrangement shown so that only three squares are left.

Now try removing two matches from the arrangement shown to leave three squares. (This time the squares need not all be the same size.)

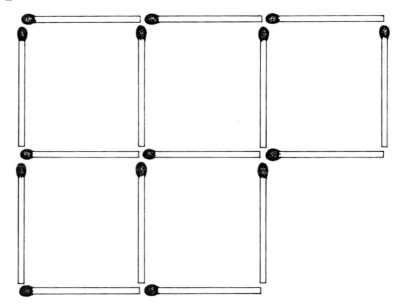

21 The square, cross and circle

Three holes are cut in a sheet of metal as shown.

How could one block of wood be cut which could pass through each hole and fit them each exactly?

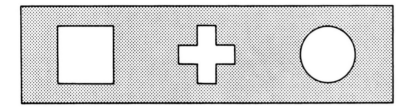

22 The baffled engine driver

The diagram shows a circular railway siding at the end of a main line.

C is a cattle truck, S is a sheep truck, E is an engine, and FB is a footbridge over the line.

The problem is to shunt the trucks so that the cattle truck and sheep truck change places and the engine is back on the main line.

The height of the footbridge is such that the engine can pass underneath but the trucks are both too high to do so.

Can you help the engine driver?

23 The ingenious milkman

A milkman has only a 5 pint jug and a 3 pint jug to measure out milk for his customers from a milk churn.

How can he measure 1 pint without wasting any milk?

24 The army's predicament

An army on the march through the jungle came to a river which was wide, deep and infested with crocodiles. On the far bank they could see two native boys with a canoe. The canoe can hold one man with his rifle and kit or two boys. How does the army cross the river?

25 Curves of constant breadth

The idea of using a roller with a circular cross-section to help in the movement of heavy objects is very old. It is believed that the Ancient Egyptians used such rollers to aid them in building the pyramids.

How far would the block above move forward when the rollers move forward 1 metre? No, the answer is not '1 metre'.

Roll a book on three pencils to discover the right answer if you cannot see it by looking at the diagram.

When a block rolls on circular rollers it moves smoothly parallel to the ground. You might think that a circle is the only possible cross-section which could be used. However, there are many shapes which have the property that when they are turned their breadth is always the same. Two such shapes are shown here.

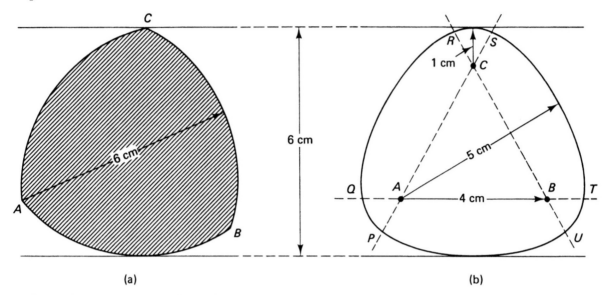

(a)　　　　　　　　　　　　(b)

Draw them onto card and cut them out.

To draw the shape in (a) take a compass and set it at 6 cm. Draw an arc with centre at A to represent the boundary BC. Now put the compass point at B and draw arc AC. Finally put the compass point at C and draw AB.

After cutting out the shape draw two parallel lines on paper 6 cm apart. Arrange your shape to touch both lines and roll it along one line (holding a ruler along one line will help). You should find that the shape will always be touching both lines no matter what angle it is turned through.

To draw the second shape in (b) start by drawing an equilateral triangle ABC whose sides are 4 cm long and then extend the sides outwards by at least 1 cm in each direction. Set your compass with a radius of 5 cm and draw arc ST from centre A, arc QR from centre B, arc UP from centre C. Now set the compass with a radius of 1 cm and draw arc PQ from centre A, arc TU from centre B, and arc RS from centre C. This shape should also be tested between two parallel lines 6 cm apart.

Now draw a square whose side is 6 cm and see that your shapes will fit inside them in such a way that they will always touch all four sides at the same time. This fact has been used in designing a special drill for cutting out square holes, as in (c).

(c)

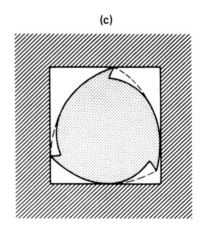

The fifty pence piece (see (d)) is also a curve of constant breadth (see if you can draw one on a larger scale), and the rotor of the revolutionary rotary engine designed by Wankel (see (e)) has the same property.

Although these shapes make very acceptable rollers they would be very unacceptable as wheels. Why? Could any other shape than a circle be used for a wheel?

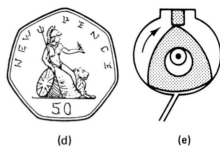

(d)   (e)

26   The Möbius band

First take a strip of paper *ABCD* about 30 cm long and 2 cm wide and join it in the form of a band as shown in (a). Make the join (sellotape is quick) without twisting the paper so that *A* meets *D* and *B* meets *C*.

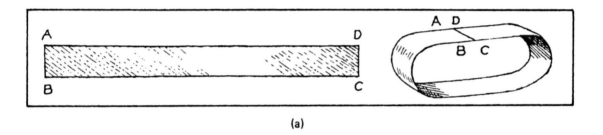

(a)

This band has two easily recognisable surfaces – colour the inside surface.

How many edges has the band?

What would happen to the band if you made a cut right along its length as shown in (b)?

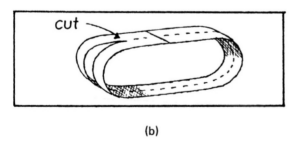

(b)

The answers to the questions so far have all been straightforward, but what follows will certainly surprise you if you have not met it before.

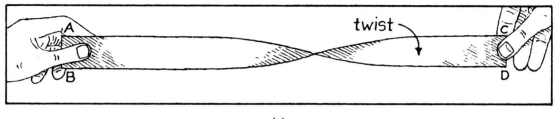

(c)

Start with another strip of paper *ABCD*. Now twist one end of the strip through 180° before joining it into a band with *A* meeting *C* and *B* meeting *D,* as shown in (d).

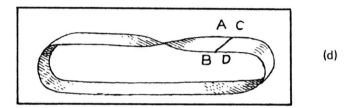

(d)

This new style band is known as a Möbius band and has many fascinating properties.

Try colouring the 'inside' of the band and you will find it only has one side. This fact is used by engineers in belts connecting pulleys. By making the belt a Möbius band the engineer ensures it will wear evenly.

How many edges has the band?

Now for another surprise! Cut along the length of the band along its middle until you come to the starting point.

What do you find? Describe the result carefully, recording the number of pieces and the number of twists.

Now make another Möbius band and cut along it, always keeping a third of the distance from the edge (see (e)). After cutting twice around the band you should come back to the starting point.

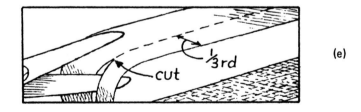

(e)

What is the result this time? Did you predict it? Again record your result carefully.

Experiment with bands having more twists and record your results.

See if you can come to any general conclusions.

27 Inside or outside

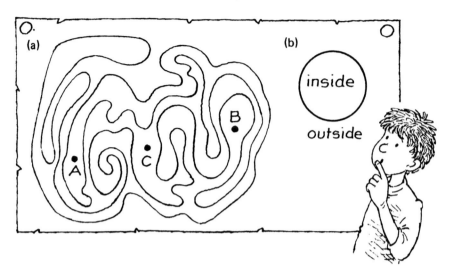

Looking at drawings (a) and (b) you may well be surprised to learn that the drawing in (a) is called a *simple* closed curve. This is because it does not cross over itself and if you imagined it as a loop of string it could be rearranged as a circle. The other property which defines this kind of curve is that it has a simple inside and outside just like the circle in (b). Which of the points *A*, *B* and *C* are inside and which outside the curve in (a)?

The simple closed curve in (c) represents an unusual prison boundary. A prisoner at *P* finds the boundary very confusing and does not realise he only has to cross the fence once to get out. Show that no matter in which direction he tries to escape he will need to cross the boundary fence an odd number of times before there is no fence in front of him. Can you explain this?

This is all very well as long as the prison boundary is on a surface like the earth, but suppose we lived on a surface like a life belt (see (d)). In this case it is possible to have circular boundaries which would not imprison anyone. Can you find such a boundary?

(d)

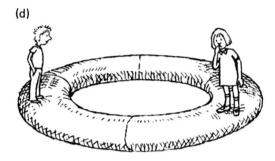

28 Rolling along

A square packing case *ABCD* is moved across the warehouse floor by first turning it about *A* until *DC* is uppermost, then about *B* etc. as shown in the diagram.

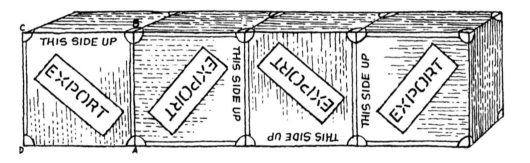

Make a careful drawing of the path followed by the point *B* as the packing case is rolled across the floor.

It may help you to cut a square piece of card to represent the packing case and roll it along the edge of a ruler.

What is the path traced out by (i) the middle point of *AB*, (ii) the centre of the square?

Investigate the paths followed by points on other shapes as they roll along a level floor.

29 Which way is the wheel moving?

If you are asked to describe the motion of the wheels shown here you will probably say they are turning around clockwise, but such a description does not say much about the direction in which different points move. In (a) the wheel is turning about a fixed axle whilst in (b) it is rolling along the ground. In (c) the wheel is designed like that of a train and rolls on a rail.

Indicate on each wheel the directions that the points A, B, C, D and O are moving at the instant shown.

Make a model out of card to help if you need it.

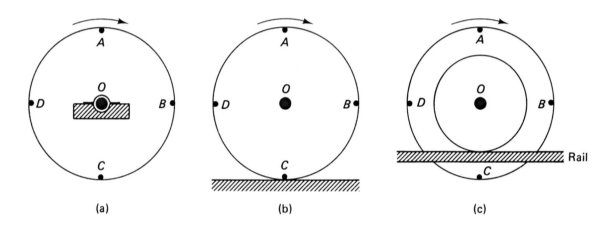

(a)   (b)   (c)

30 Gear trains

Many mechanisms use a train of gear wheels to transmit motion from one rotating shaft to another. The diagrams below give some examples. The number on each gear wheel gives the number of teeth. In each case decide in which direction and through what angle B turns when A makes one complete turn clockwise.

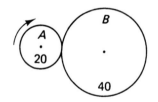

B turns anticlockwise through half a turn.

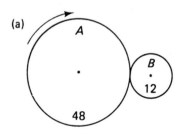

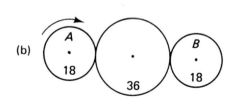

22

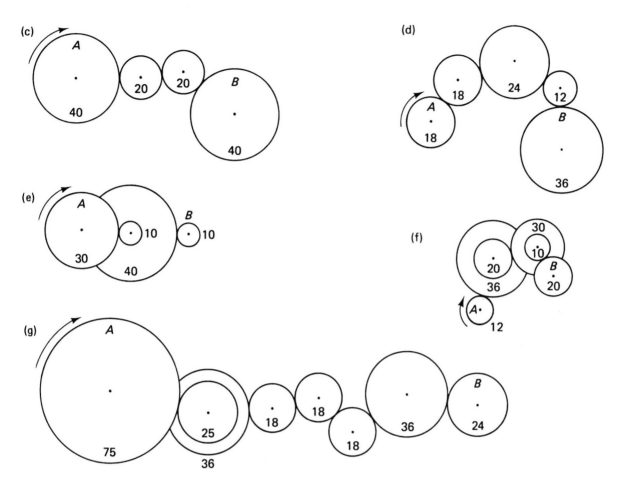

Have you spotted the rules which govern gear trains?

Investigate the gear trains in such mechanisms as: a hand drill, an egg whisk, a clock, a winch, a food mixer, a toy.

Sometimes the output shaft is geared to turn faster than the input shaft, sometimes the reverse.

Suppose that you had available gear wheels with 60 teeth, 36 teeth, 12 teeth and 24 teeth. Design gear trains

(i) where the output shaft turns 6 times as fast as the input shaft.

(ii) where the output shaft turns only $\frac{1}{15}$ times as fast as the input shaft.

(iii) which would correctly link the movements of the minute hand and the hour hand of a clock.

How could you modify your gear trains to reverse the direction of motion of the output shafts?

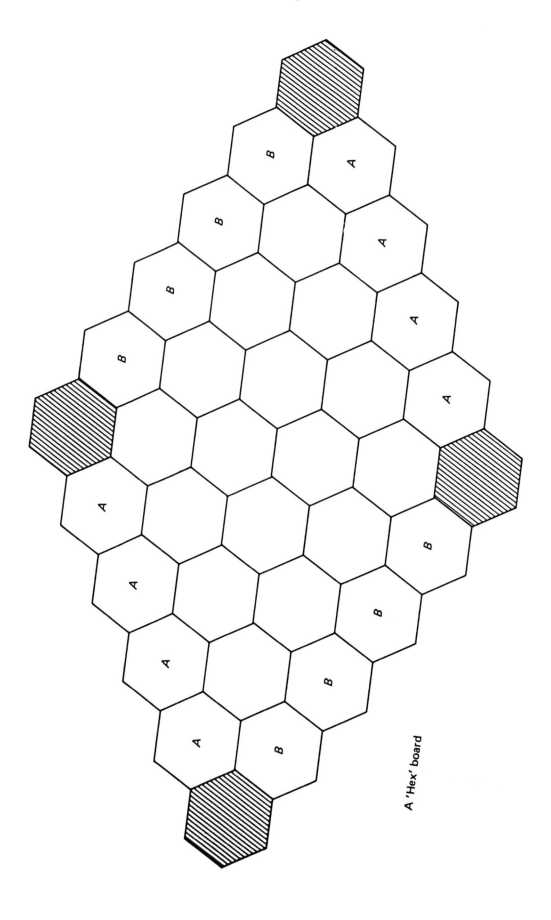

A 'Hex' board

31 Hex

Hex is a board game which was invented in 1942 by Piet
Hein, a Danish mathematician. A typical board, shown here,
is diamond (rhombus) shaped and is made up of interlocking
hexagons. This one has six hexagons on each edge, to start
you off, but experts play the game on a board which has
eleven hexagons along each edge.

One player has a supply of black counters, the other a
supply of white counters. (Any small identifiable objects
will do, e.g. buttons, coloured pegs, drawing pins, Smarties.)
The players take it in turn to put one of their counters
on any unoccupied hexagon. The object of play is to complete a continuous chain of counters from one edge of the
board to the opposite edge. 'Black' plays from *A* to *A* while
'white' plays from *B* to *B*. Each player, as well as trying to
complete his own chain, naturally tries to block his opponent's attempts.

Drawings (a) and (b) show the results of two games.

Note that the corner hexagons can either be excluded, or
counted as being on the edge for both players.

There is more to this game than first appears. Challenge
your friends. Have fun, and make yourself a larger board!

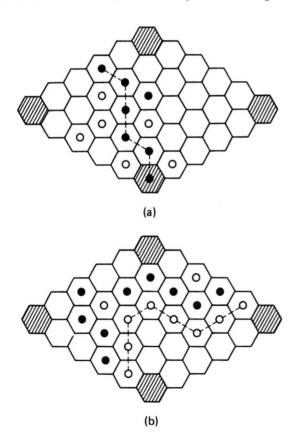

(a)

(b)

32 The knight's dance

Two white knights and two black knights are placed at the corners of a 3 x 3 square on a chessboard as shown.

How can you make the white knights change places with the black knights in the fewest number of moves?

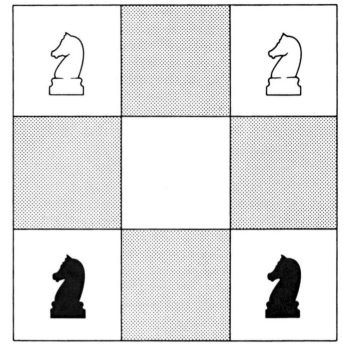

33 The railway sidings

A railway line BC has two very short sidings BA and CA. In each siding is a single truck, labelled T_1 and T_2 in the diagram. On the main line BC is an engine. You have to decide how to use the engine to shunt the trucks so that they change places and the engine can return to the main line. Before trying, however, note that the portion of the rails at A common to the two sidings is only long enough for a single truck such as T_1 or T_2, but is too short for the engine, so that if the engine travels in along CA it cannot come out along AB. Trucks can be linked to each other or to either end of the engine, but bouncing off the buffers at A is not allowed!

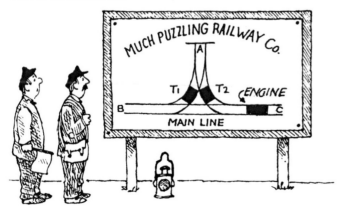

34 The multi-coloured cube

Imagine you have eight wooden one-centimetre cubes. Show how they could be painted so that they could be fitted together to make either a red two-centimetre cube or a blue two-centimetre cube.

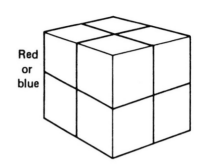

Red or blue

Now consider the similar problem with 27 one-centimetre cubes. Can you colour the cubes in such a way that they could be assembled into a red three-centimetre, a blue three-centimetre cube or a yellow three-centimetre cube?

35 The jealous husbands

After a flood three married couples found themselves surrounded by water, and had to escape from their holiday hotel in a boat that would only hold three persons at a time. Each husband was so jealous that he would not allow his wife to be in the boat or on either bank with any other man (or men) unless he was himself present.

Find a way of getting the couples across the water to safety which requires the smallest number of boat crossings. Swimming or helicopters are not allowed!

Now solve the problem if there are five married couples.

36 The extension lead

A room is 30 ft long, 12 ft wide and 12 ft high. There is a 13 amp power point at *A* in the middle of an end wall 1 ft from the floor. An extension lead is required to connect *A* with a point *B* in the middle of the opposite wall but 1 ft from the ceiling.

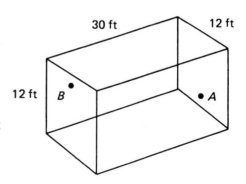

For safety the lead must be fastened to the surfaces of the room and not stretch across the middle. Find the shortest length of cable needed to do the job. No, the answer is not 42 ft.

37 The economical gardener

A gardener liked to make the most of the plants he had and one day he found, when laying out a rose bed, that he had managed to plant seven rose bushes in such a way that they formed six lines with three rose bushes in each line. How did he do it?

Pleased with himself the gardener looked for other interesting arrangements until he found a way of planting ten rose bushes so that he had five lines with four rose bushes in each line.

Find his arrangements.

Investigate other 'economic' arrangements.

38 Perimeter and area

Make as many shapes as you can on a pinboard which have a perimeter of 12 units.

Record each new shape on spotty paper.

The two examples shown both have an area of 5 square units. Find the area of each of your shapes.

There is a triangle with a perimeter of 12 units which can be made.

What other non-rectangular shapes are possible?

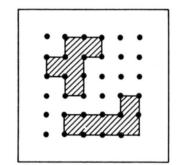

39 Tessellations

The shaded quadrilateral is shown repeated to form a tiling pattern.

Make up tiling patterns using the other shapes given.

Find new shapes which will form tiling patterns.

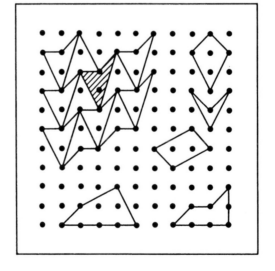

40 Tessellations and art

The artist M. C. Escher has made a fascinating study of ways
in which tessellations become transformed into objects and
living things such as birds and fish. By starting with a simple
tessellation of rectangles or quadrilaterals, try systematically
modifying it into a repeating pattern of some recognisable
form.

 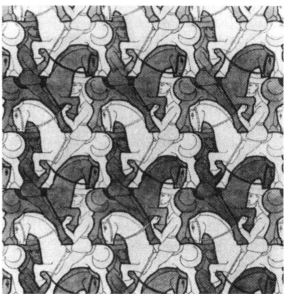

41 Shapes with the same area

Explain why the shaded shapes have an area of 2 units when
the unit of area is that of one square on a pinboard.

Find on a 3 × 3 pinboard as many different shapes as you
can whose area is 2 units. Record your shapes on spotty paper.

How would your answer be different on a 5 × 5 pinboard?

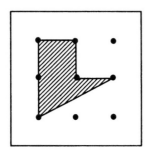 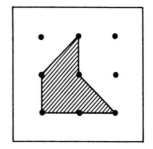

42   Area on a pinboard

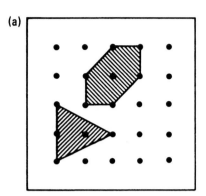

The two shapes shown on the 5 × 5 pinboard (a) each contain 1 pin inside them.

Make and record other shapes which have only 1 pin inside them.

Find the area (A) of each shape and a formula relating A to the number of pins (b) on the boundary of the shape.

The shape shown on pinboard (b) has 12 pins on its boundary and 1 pin inside itself.

Find shapes with 12 boundary pins and 0, 1, 2, 3, 4, 5, 6, 7, 8, . . . points inside itself. Is there any limit to the number of interior pins when the boundary contains 12 pins?

Find a formula relating the area (A) of shapes with 12 boundary pins to the number of interior pins (i).

There is a relation, known as Pict's theorem, which gives the area (A) of any polygon which can be formed on a pinboard in terms of the number of its boundary pins (b) and the number of pins on its inside (i).

Use the results you have obtained so far to try to discover Pict's theorem. Test your guess on a new polygon.

(b)

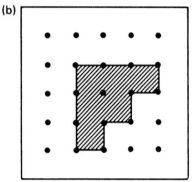

43   Routes on a pinboard

(a)

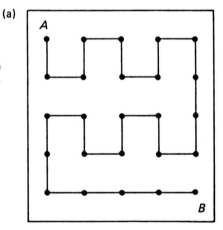

Diagram (a) shows a 5 × 5 pinboard with a band from A to B which 'visits' each pin once. (No diagonal routes are allowed.) See what other routes you can find of the same kind. Are any routes symmetric?

What can you say about the length of such routes? Generalise for an n × n board.

Now consider the possible routes from A to B on a 3 × 3 board where diagonal routes are allowed and all pins have to be visited once only (as in (b), for example).

Find (i) the shortest and (ii) the longest such route if the route is not allowed to cross itself.

What is the longest route when the route can cross itself? Now try this with a 5 × 5 board.

(b)

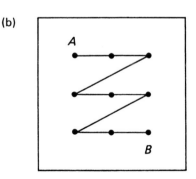

44 Zigzag

Use a 7 x 7 or 9 x 9 square array of dots.

Start at the centre dot, S.

The first player draws an arrow either across or up and down to the nearest dot.

The second player follows with an arrow to form a continuous path.

The players move alternately. The object is to form a path from S to the home base (A for the first player, B for the second player) without visiting any point more than once. The first player to home base wins.

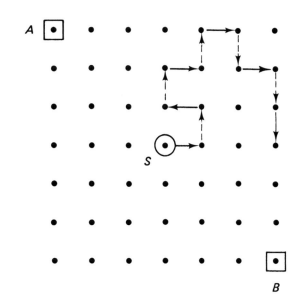

45 How many triangles can you make?

How many triangles can be made on a 3 x 3 pinboard?

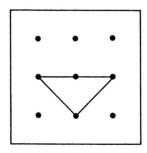

46 How many triangles can you see?

The figure contains many triangles, some of which overlap each other.

Make a copy of the diagram and find a systematic way of accounting for all the triangles.

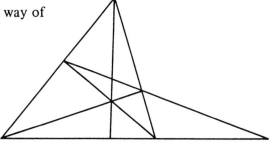

47 The unfriendly power-boats

Two radio-controlled power-boats are moored 200 metres
apart at A and B near the centre of a large lake. The boats
are both controlled by the same radio transmitter in such a
way that they move at the same speed. However, the boat
which leaves B has a faulty steering mechanism and moves on
a bearing which is always 90° more than the bearing of the
boat which leaves A. How can the controller steer the boats
to meet each other?

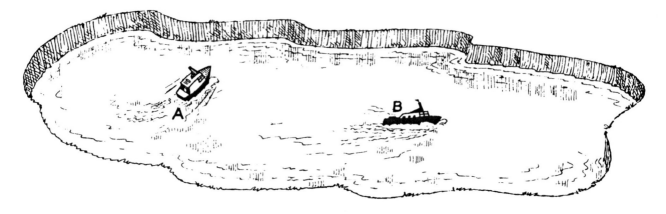

48 Traversibility

Drawing (a) is a map of a road network. A road engineer
starting at A wants to travel along each road once only and
return to A. How can he do it?

Network (b) cannot be traced out with a pencil unless you
go over some lines twice or take your pencil off the paper
and start at another point.
Find the smallest number of times you need to take your
pencil off the paper to draw it.

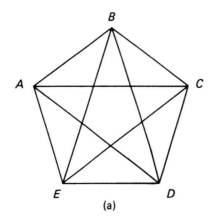

(a)

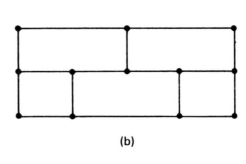

(b)

49 The knight-guards

Show how to place twelve
knights on a chessboard so
that every square is either
occupied or attacked.

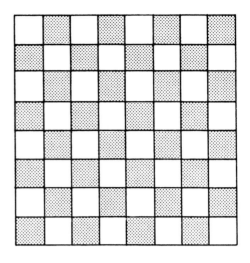

50 Reversing the trains

The diagram shows the plan
of the rail network in a large
town. Each small circle is a
station and each number refers
to a train. The station at the
bottom has no train.

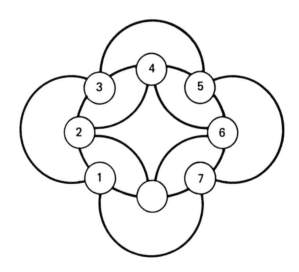

By moving one train at a time to the station left empty,
show how to move the trains so that their order is reversed.
That is, 1 is in the position of 7, 2 in the position of 6 and
so on.

The first move must be made by either 1, 2, 7 or 6.

The reversal of the trains' order can be made in as few as
fifteen moves.

51 The parallelogram linkage

For this activity and the following ones you require some
strips of stiff card, brass paper fasteners, drawing pins and a
drawing board. (Geostrips or Meccano strips if available would
be ideal.)

Fasten two equal strips DA and CB to a longer strip AB
using brass paper fasteners, and then use drawing pins to pin
the ends D and C to a drawing board so that $ABCD$ is a
parallelogram. Make sure that the strips can rotate freely
about A, B, C and D.

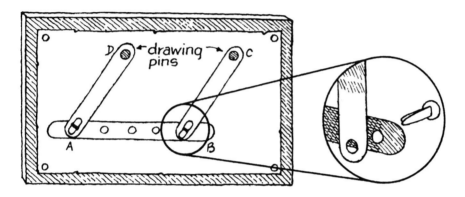

Move the linkage and describe the motion of the rod AB.

What is the path traced out by A?

Put a pencil in a hole in the strip between A and B and
trace its path. How does it compare with the path of A?

When AD turns through an angle of $30°$ what angle does
BC turn through?

These questions may seem easy but their answers give the
main properties of a parallelogram and underly the reason that
it occurs as the basis of hundreds of different mechanism where
it is important to keep one part moving parallel to another. The
following illustrations give a selection of these mechanisms.
Look at them and see if you can decide why the parallel
motion is necessary in each case.

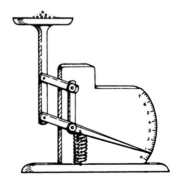

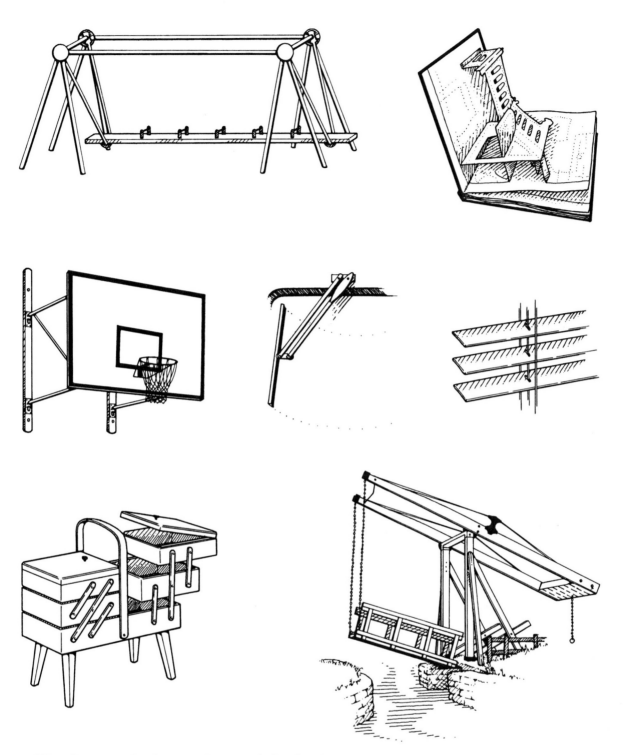

Why, for example, do some buses and diesel trains have a parallelogram linkage connecting their windscreen wiper instead of the simpler mechanism seen on most cars? Make models and compare the way in which the windscreen is swept.
Try designing a pop-up card.

52 Rocking horses

Children's rocking horses have been designed to supposedly simulate the motion of a horse in principally two ways. One way is to have curved runners while the other way is to use a trapezium linkage.

Make up the trapezium linkage shown right as in the previous activity using card strips, drawing pins and paper fasteners on a drawing board. Now move AB to and fro and observe its motion. As AB moves to the right from the position shown A moves upwards while B moves downwards, thus giving AB a rocking motion. The 'Tom Cobley' rocking horses seen in children's playgrounds are based on this mechanism. The points D and C correspond to the tops of two posts fixed in the ground and two bars are connected to these points and to points A and B which are in the body of the horse to form a trapezium $ABCD$.

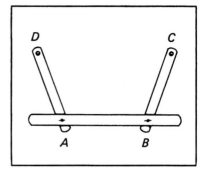

You can make an attractive working model of a Tom Cobley out of card and fasten D and C to a piece of card using paper fasteners. Make the body of the horse large enough to hide the strips AD and BC and the result should intrigue your friends.

How does the motion of a Tom Cobley compare with that of a real horse or with that of a rocking horse on runners?

Without access to the cinefilm of a horse it is difficult to compare the motion of a real horse to a toy one but it is certainly possible, by making models, to compare the effect of a trapezium linkage with that of a horse on runners.

Start with the model of a trapezium linkage and see if you can design a horse on runners to give the same motion.

Rocking chairs have traditionally been designed using curved runners but for anyone with a practical bent there should be now no problem in designing one based on a trapezium linkage which should be smoother in operation and less damaging to the floor covering!

53 Turning circles

Cars are designed to be manoeuvered in congested spaces. To do this they must be able to turn in a relatively small circle, but this would create considerable tyre wear unless the steering mechanism had been carefully thought out. In the diagram on the right the car is turning about the point O. For a wheel to roll smoothly over the ground without being dragged sideways then it must roll in a direction which is at right-angles to the line drawn from O to its centre. This can only be achieved if the front wheels A and B do not remain parallel to one another as the driver turns the car. The angle θ between the wheels A and B will depend on the radius of the turning circle and increase as the radius becomes smaller.

Interestingly the mechanism to bring this about is the same trapezium linkage used in the rocking horse design. Make up a model from card and pin to a drawing board as shown here. Move CD to the left and observe that as the wheels A and B turn to the right they cease to be parallel.

The lengths of AB and DC depend on the wheel base of the car. Investigate. The actual mechanism is not so easy to observe on a car but take a look at a farm tractor next time you see one.

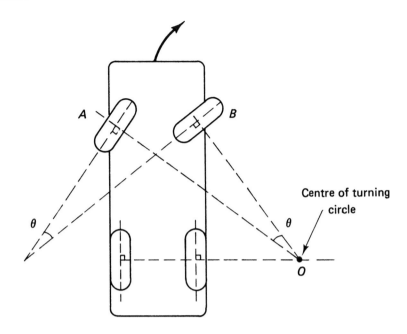

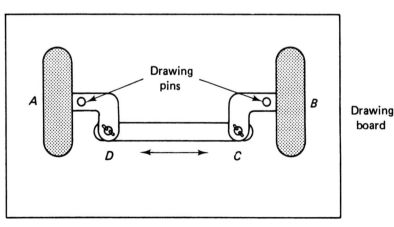

54 Straight-line motion – well almost!

At the end of the eighteenth century and throughout much of the nineteenth century the industrial revolution saw a proliferation of mechanisms. Many of these were associated with the development of the steam engine. One significant design problem for the engineers was to produce a mechanism to give straight-line motion which involved as small a friction as possible. Their many solutions might not have satisfied a pure mathematician because they did not give exact straight lines, but they worked which was what mattered in practice.

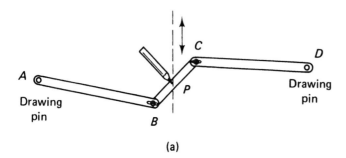

(a)

James Watt came up with one of the first practical solutions in 1784. He used two long equal bars AB and CD and a much shorter bar joining them (see (a)). A and D are fixed pivots and as the linkage is moved up and down P, the middle point of BC, follows a path which appears to be a straight line. However, as you move BC as far as it will go and trace out the complete path of P you will see it is far from a straight line!

A good example of this linkage, which is known as Watt's parallel motion, can be seen at the York Railway Museum on a large steam engine which was originally used for hauling loaded trucks up an incline.

In 1850 Tchebycheff produced a somewhat similar linkage to approximate to straight-line motion. In this case the rods *AB* and *CD* are of equal length and cross over each other (see (b)). The distances *BC* and *AD* are such that

$AB : BC : AD = 5 : 2 : 4$

Make the linkage using card strips and trace out the path followed by *P*, the middle point of *BC*, using a pencil.

To find the complete path you will need to ensure that the strips overlap as shown to allow the linkage to move freely from its crossed configuration to its uncrossed configuration.

Investigate the different paths which are formed by taking longer strips for *BC*.

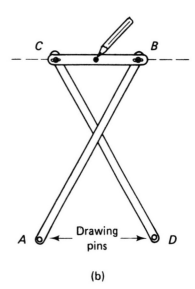

(b)

55 About turn

One of the simplest transformations which can be made to a shape is to turn it through an angle of 180° about a point. This can be brought about by a variety of linkages. Drawings (a), (b) and (c) illustrate three such linkages all based on rhombuses. To make them you need two sizes of strips, one size to be twice the length of the other.

In each case fix point *A* to a drawing board. Draw an object shape such as *S*, then guide *P* around the boundary of *S*.

You will find that point *Q* will trace out a path *S'*, which is the image of *S* after a 180° rotation about *A*.

Try to design other linkages which will produce the same result.

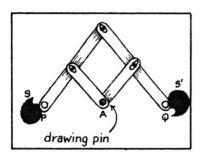

(a)

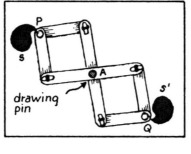

(b)

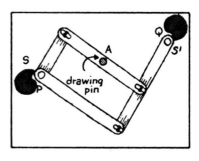

(c)

The complicated looking linkage in (d) is the result of joining two half-turn linkages together. A and B are fixed pivots. As P traces out the shape S, Q will trace out S' its half-turn image about A, and R will then trace out S'' the half-turn image of S' about B.

The result is a translation of S to S'' of twice the translation from A to B.

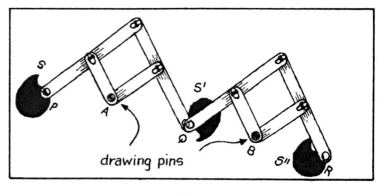

drawing pins

(d)

56 Knight lines

This is a game based on the knight's move in chess and on noughts and crosses. You can play the game with pencils on squared paper or use coloured counters on a squared board or pegs on a pegboard.

The game is played on a 5 x 5 board as shown.

The first player marks a nought (labelled O_1 in the example shown in (a)), and the second player then marks a cross (X_2) which is a knight's move from the last square played in by the first player. The first player now marks a nought (O_3) in a square which is a knight's move from X_2. Play continues with the players alternately, adding a nought or a cross a knight's move from the previous play until no further move is possible. Diagram (a) shows the state of play after six moves of a game.

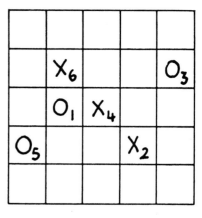

(a)

The object of the game is to obtain lines of circles and crosses and accumulate as many points as possible given that

three circles in a line score   1 point,
four circles in a line score   2 points,
five circles in a line score   3 points.

Similarly for crosses. Diagram (b) shows an example.

In addition the player who plays last earns a bonus point.

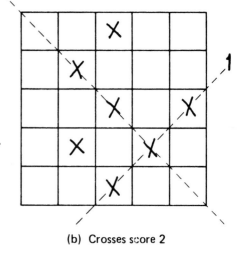

(b) Crosses score 2

Diagrams (c)–(f) show some typical games. The squares
have been numbered so that you can follow the play.

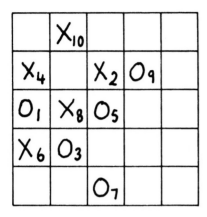

Diagram (c):

	X_{10}			
X_4		X_2	O_9	
O_1	X_8	O_5		
X_6	O_3			
		O_7		

Diagram (d):

			O_9	X_{14}
	X_{10}	O_7		
	O_1	X_4	O_{13}	X_8
O_3		O_{11}	X_6	
	O_5	X_2		X_{12}

(c) *A 2–2 draw*
Circles: two lines of 3   2 points
Crosses: X_{10} the last move 1 point
             one line of 3   1 point

(d) *A 3–4 win for crosses*
Circles: one line of 4   2 points
             one line of 3   1 point
Crosses: X_{14} the last move 1 point
             one line of 4   2 points
             one line of 3   1 point

Diagram (e):

O_3		O_{11}		O_5
X_8		X_4		X_{10}
	X_2	O_9	X_6	
	O_7			
O_1				

Diagram (f):

		O_7		O_{13}
	O_3	X_{12}		X_8
O_{11}		O_1	X_6	
X_2		X_4	O_9	
	X_{10}			O_5

(e) *A 2–0 win for circles*
Circles: O_{11} the last move 1 point
             one line of 3   1 point

(f) *A 4–2 win for circles*
Circles: O_{13} the last move 1 point
             one line of 4   2 points
             one line of 3   1 point
Crosses: one line of 4   2 points

This game was originally devised with a group of children
at a mathematics club who had been challenged to develop a
game from noughts and crosses. They enjoyed playing the
game. Try playing it yourself and then see if you can invent
one.

57 Quadruplets

Show how the shape on the
right can be divided into
four pieces which are identical
to each other.

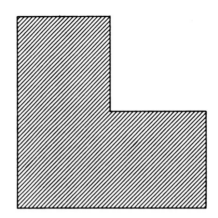

58 Complete the square

Carefully draw the five shapes
shown here on squared paper.
Cut them out and then show
how they can be put together
to form a square. Do not
despair – it is possible!

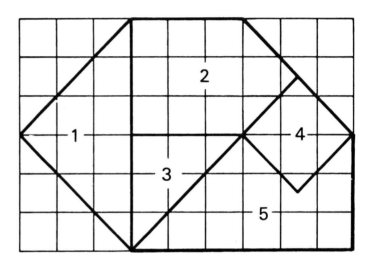

59 Roll a penny

A penny *A* is rolled around a
second penny *B* without
slipping until it returns to its
starting point.

How many revolutions
does penny *A* make?

A   B

60 The hunter

A hunter followed his prey 3 miles south, 3 miles east and then eventually shot it after stalking it for another 3 miles which took him back to the point where he started.

    What was his prey?

61 Four points in a plane

Mark four points on a flat surface so that there are only two different distances between them.

    One arrangement is shown. There are five other possible arrangements. Find them!

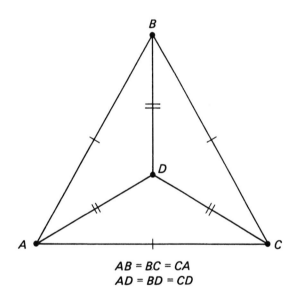

AB = BC = CA
AD = BD = CD

62 The letter dice

A word game uses dice with a letter on each face. Three views of one of the dice are shown above. Which letter is on the face opposite H?

63 Make yourself a hexaflexagon

A hexaflexagon is an intriguing arrangement of equilateral triangles folded in such a way that at any time six of them form a hexagon. The flexagon can be 'flexed' into a new arrangement by pinching together two adjacent triangles and opening out the triangles from the centre to reveal a new face. When you have made a flexagon mark the corners of the triangles at the centre of the visible hexagon with a symbol such as a heart or diamond, or spell out a six letter word. Then flex the hexaflexagon and mark the centre of the new face with another set of symbols. You will be surprised just how many different centres you can find! With a lot of patience you could stick parts of a picture like a jigsaw to the centre cut from a christmas card for example.

 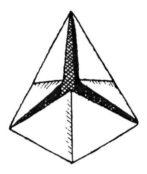 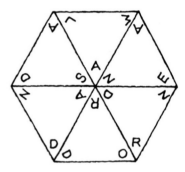

Now for the method of construction.

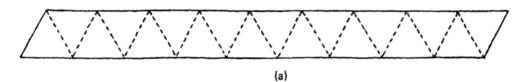

(a)

On a strip of thin card draw eighteen equilateral triangles as in (a). You will find 5 cm a good size for the side of a triangle.

Score along each of the dotted sides of the triangles. On one side number the triangles 1, 2, 3, 1, 2, 3, . . . , and mark the end triangles along the edge as in (b).

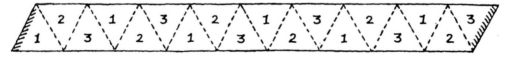

(b)

Turn the strip over and number the other side with a 4, 4,
5, 5, 6, 6, . . . pattern exactly like diagram (c).

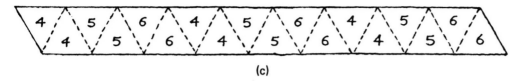

(c)

Next fold the strip by placing triangle 4 onto triangle 4, 5
onto 5, 6 onto 6 etc., as in (d). This rolls the strip up (see (e)).

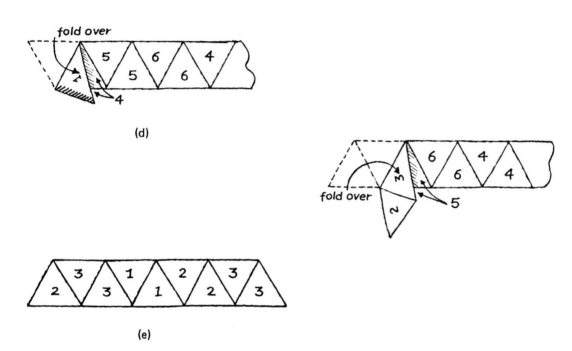

(d)

(e)

Now fold the strip again so that triangles of the same
number are all on top, as shown in (f).

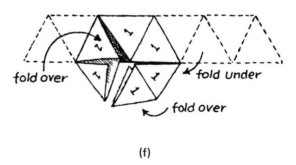

(f)

Stick the two marked edges together using sellotape.

64 Perigal's dissection

Pythagoras' well-known theorem for a right-angled triangle
ABC states that the area of the square on the hypotenuse AC
is equal to the sum of the areas of the squares on the other
two sides AB and BC.

A nice demonstration of this result was shown by Perigal
and can be reconstructed as follows.

First draw a right-angled triangle ABC and then carefully
draw a square on each side as shown above.

Find the centre of square $ABDE$ by drawing in its diagonals
(shown dotted). Now divide the square into four equal pieces
by drawing lines XY and UV through the centre and parallel to
the sides of the square on AC.

Cut the square $ABDE$ into the four pieces marked and fit
them into the corners of the square on AC. They leave a
square in the middle exactly the same size as the square on
BC.

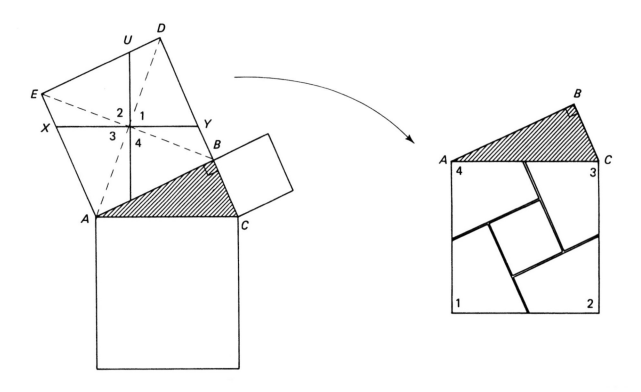

65 Make a tetrahedron to baffle your friends

Imagine a tetrahedron (i.e. a triangular-based pyramid) sliced into equal parts as shown in (a). The points A, B, C and D are the middle points of the edges in each case.

The tetrahedron shown is regular which means that all its faces are equilateral triangles and the cut face $ABCD$ will be a square.

You may have come across the half-tetrahedron shapes as a puzzle in a Christmas cracker or elsewhere, for the interesting thing is that when someone is given the two halves and invited to put them together to make a tetrahedron they frequently find it impossible to do.

To make the half-tetrahedron shapes you will need some card.

A possible net for the shape is shown in (b).

Start by constructing an equilateral triangle ABC whose side is 18 cm. By marking off points at 6 cm intervals most of the net is easily constructed – only the square remains to be added at the top.

Before cutting out mark the tabs (shown shaded) and score all the fold lines with a compass point. (To make an identical net for the other half use a compass point and prick through the corners of the net you have drawn onto a second piece of card.) Cut out and fold up the net to form the required shape. A quick-drying glue such as UHU is an advantage although you may prefer sellotape.

(a)

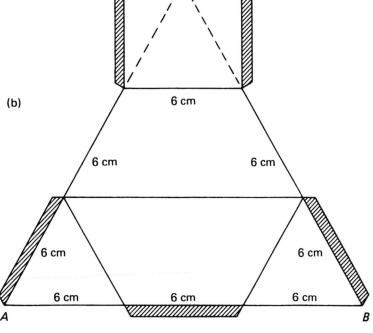

(b)

47

66 The cone which rolls uphill

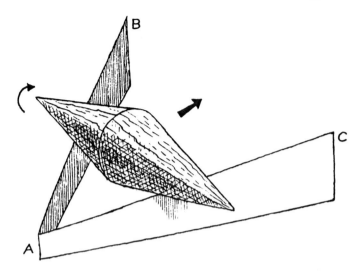

When a double cone is placed on two rails *AB* and *AC* as shown it will appear to roll uphill.

The fact is that although the rails slope upwards they become further apart so the parts of the cones in contact with the rails are nearer to their points with the effect that the centre of the double cone becomes lower as the cone rolls 'up' the rails.

Ideally this works best with a heavy wood or metal cone (do you know someone with a lathe?) but it will work if you make the cones from card.

Cut out two quarter-circles from card – the larger the better – and make them into a double cone. The rails can then be made from card or a couple of rulers suitably fixed. If it does not work at first make the rails less steep and/or increase the size of the angle between them.

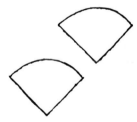

67 Ruler and compass constructions

To bisect a line AB (see (a)) take a compass with centre at
A and radius greater than half AB and draw an arc. Next,
with the same radius but with centre at B draw an arc to cut
the first arc at X and Y. Join XY. The point M where XY
cuts AB is the middle of AB.

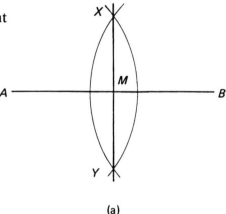

(a)

To bisect an angle PQR (see (b)) take a compass and draw an
arc with centre Q to cut PQ in S and RQ in T. Next with
centre at T and a radius larger than half TS, draw an arc. With
the same radius but with centre at S now draw an arc to cut
the last arc drawn at Z. Join QZ. The line QZ bisects the
angle PQR.

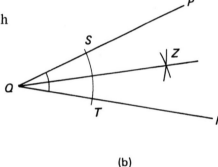

(b)

*To draw a line from a point A which is perpendicular to a
line l* (see (c)) take a compass and draw an arc with centre
at A to cut the line l in two points X and Y. With centre at
X and radius larger than half XY, draw an arc. Use the same
radius and centre Y to draw an arc to cut the last arc drawn
at W. Join AW. The line AW is then the line from A perpendicular to l.

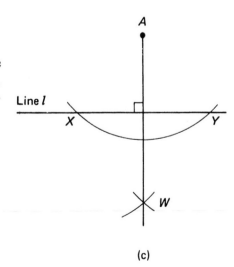

(c)

To construct an equilateral triangle (see (d)) take a point *A* as centre and with any convenient radius draw an arc, α. Take a point *B* on the arc as centre and with the same radius draw an arc β from *A* until it meets arc α at *C*. As a check now take *C* as centre and with the same radius you should be able to draw an arc γ from *A* to *B*. Triangle *ABC* is then equilateral whose side length is equal to the radius of the compass.

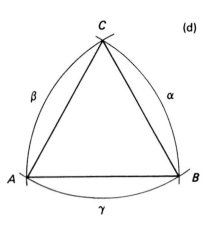

Now try to construct the following:

    (i) a square,   (iii) a regular octagon,
   (ii) a regular hexagon,   (iv) angles of $45°$, $30°$, $75°$, $52\frac{1}{2}°$.

68 Circumscribed, inscribed and escribed circles

Here you can see how to construct a very special set of circles associated with triangles.

The circumscribed circle

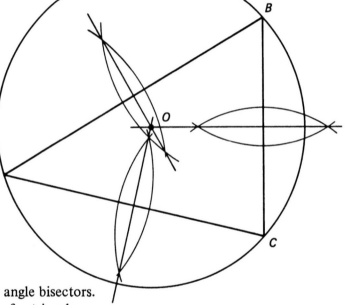

Draw a triangle *ABC*, preferably one whose angles are all acute, and carefully construct the bisectors of each side. They should all meet at the same point *O*. If they do not start again, make sure your pencil is sharp and that all your lines go through the intersections precisely. Now put your compass point at *O* and you will be able to draw the unique circle which goes through *A*, *B* and *C* known as the circumscribed circle for triangle *ABC*.

Where is *O* if the triangle has (i) a right-angle, (ii) an obtuse angle?

The inscribed circle

Draw a triangle *PQR* and construct its three angle bisectors. These should meet in a point *I*, the in-centre for triangle *PQR*. Put your compass point at *I* and adjust the radius of the compass so that you can draw a circle which just touches each of the sides of triangle *PQR*. This is its inscribed circle.

Both these centres described so far could equally well be found by folding the paper to find the bisecting lines – try this yourself.

50

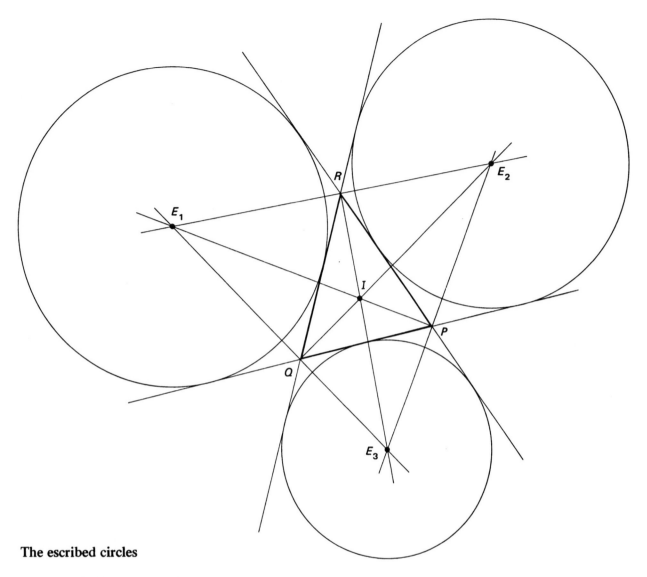

The escribed circles

At first this diagram may look very complicated, but it can
be thought of as an extension of the previous one for drawing the inscribed circle. Start in the same way but with
triangle *PQR* near the centre of your paper and of a size to
leave plenty of space around it for the additional circles.
Extend the sides of triangle *PQR* outward in both directions
as in the diagram. The point E_1 is found by extending the
bisector of the interior angle at *P*, and by constructing QE_1
and RE_1, the bisectors of the exterior angles at *Q* and *R*.
When you have found E_1 use it as the centre for a new
circle which touches the sides of *PQR* as shown. This is one
of the three *escribed* circles for the triangle. Now construct
the other two.

   You will need to be very accurate at all stages if you are
to end up with a satisfactory drawing but it is well worth
the care required.

69 Submarines, cruisers and helicopters

This is a three-dimensional game for two players based on the familiar 'Battleships and Cruisers' game.

Each player has

 (i)   three 4 × 4 boards corresponding to his territory underwater, on the water surface, and in the air;

 (ii) an armed force consisting of three submarines, two cruisers and six helicopters.

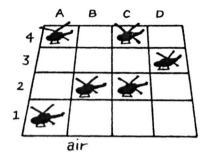

air

The ships and helicopters are represented by pieces of card or counters of such a size that when placed on the boards

a submarine occupies 2 squares,

a cruiser occupies 3 squares,

a helicopter occupies 1 square.

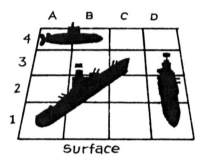

Surface

A submarine may be underwater or on the surface, but the cruisers are always on the surface and the helicopters in the air space. The diagrams above show one arrangement of a player's pieces at the beginning of a game.

The *object* of the game is for a player to destroy his opponent's forces.

The *winner* is the first player to destroy all his opponent's forces or, if the game is stopped short of this, the player who has destroyed the more. In this case a helicopter counts as 1, a submarine as 2 and a cruiser as 3.

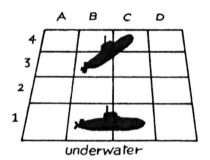

underwater

Players take it in turn to play (toss a coin to decide who starts), and when they play they have the options of

 (i)   carrying out two strikes;

 (ii) moving a piece and carrying out one strike;

(iii) moving two pieces.

A *strike* consists of naming a particular square (e.g. surface B3) and a hit results if an opponent's piece occupies that square. When a helicopter is hit the piece is taken off the board and given to the opponent. A cruiser and a submarine are not surrendered (and do not count in an unfinished game) until they have been hit in two places, but any hit has to be acknowledged (e.g. 'cruiser hit in the stern').

Note also the general point, that two pieces can never occupy the same square.

Make yourself some boards (draw three boards on a rectangular piece of card) and pieces, and challenge your friends (foes!) to a game.

The *movement of a piece* at any one time is restricted as follows:

A helicopter may move to any one of its adjacent squares in the air space as long as it is not already occupied (see diagram (a)).

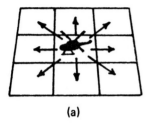

(a)

A submarine may move in three ways:
(i)   turn through an angle of 45° about one end (see diagrams (b) and (c));
(ii) change its level from water to surface or vice versa;
(iii) move one square along its length.

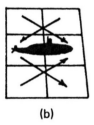

(b)

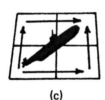

(c)

A cruiser may move in two ways:
(i)   turn through an angle of 45° about one end (see diagrams (d) and (e)) as long as no other piece is in its way;
(ii) move one square along its length.

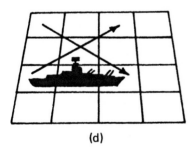

(d)

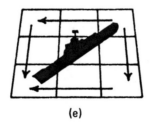

(e)

When you have mastered this game see if you can improve on it modifying the rules. Better, design your own three-dimensional game based on Star Wars, say!

70 The queen's defence

What is the smallest number of queens which can be put on an $n \times n$ chessboard so as to occupy or command all the squares on a board?

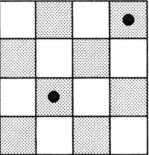

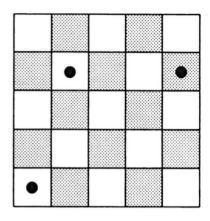

Here is a solution for the 4 x 4 board with two queens and a solution for the 5 x 5 boards with three queens.

Find other solutions for the 4 x 4 and 5 x 5 boards and then find a solution for the 6 x 6 board with three queens.

How many queens are needed when $n = 7$ and $n = 8$?

In 1862 Jaenisch proposed a variation on this problem in which not only were all squares to be occupied or commanded, but no queen was to be on a square which was under attack by another.

A related problem would be to find the smallest number of queens which would occupy or command every square subject to the restriction that every queen was protected by another.

Clearly similar problems could be set for the other chess pieces.

71 Seeing is believing

Cut out the shapes drawn on the 8 x 8 square and rearrange to form the 13 x 5 rectangle.

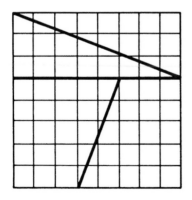

This means   64 = 65.   Where is the catch?

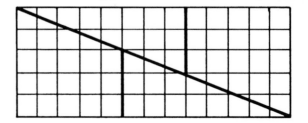

72 Inspecting the roads

The plan shows the road network connecting nine villages.
The numbers refer to the
mileages along the roads.

A council workman living
at village *A* wants to inspect
all the roads in a car. What
is the shortest route he can
take if he has to return to *A*?

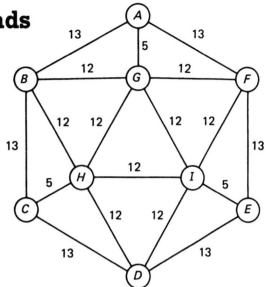

73 Dominoes on a chessboard

A domino is the same shape
and size as two squares on a
chessboard.

It is easy to see how to
place 32 such dominoes on
a chessboard so as to cover
it.

Can you decide however
if it is possible to cover the
board shown here, with the
squares at two opposite
corners missing, with 31 such
dominoes?

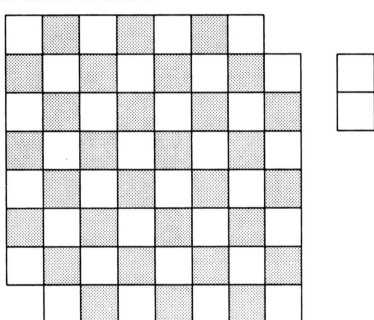

74 Identical twins

Divide shapes *X* and *Y* into two equal pieces.

Make a similar puzzle yourself.

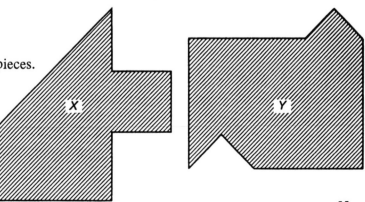

55

75 The four-colour theorem

How many colours are needed to colour a map so that any regions which have part of their boundary in common must be of a different colour? (Two regions with a point in common may be the same colour.)

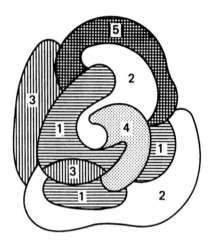

The map shown here appears to require five colours as it has been shaded but it can be coloured in using only four colours. How?

For as long as map making has been practised the map makers have believed that the different regions on a map could always be coloured using only four colours. Mathematicians have been trying to prove this result since Möbius mentioned it in a lecture in 1840. However, it defied proof until in 1978 two American mathematicians used a powerful computer to analyse the situation. But many people still have a sneaking feeling that someone will turn up with a map which cannot be coloured with as few as four colours . . . can you find one?

76 The pentominoes

Five squares can be fitted together edge-to-edge in twelve different ways. These shapes are known as the *pentominoes* and are shown here fitted together like a jigsaw to form a 10 x 6 rectangle.

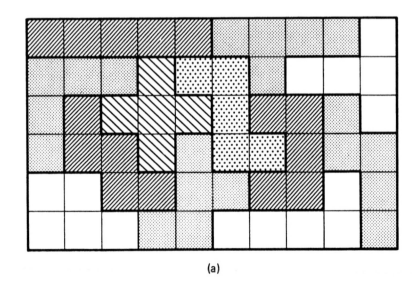

(a)

Cut yourself a set of pentominoes from thick card and see if you can find other ways of fitting them together to form 10 x 6, 12 x 5, 15 x 4 and 20 x 3 rectangles. There are thousands of solutions altogether but you can be congratulated if you find one of each shape.

One of the pentomino shapes can form a regular repeating pattern to cover the page without any gaps (that is it forms a *tessellation* – see (b)). Draw patterns to show which of the other pentominoes will tessellate.

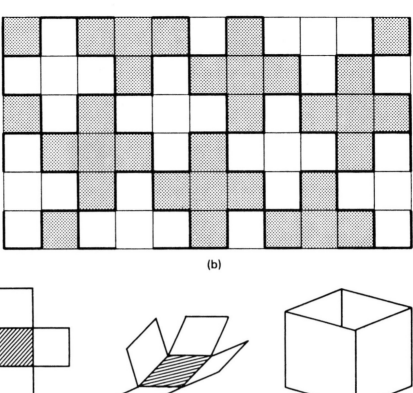

(b)

(c)

The same pentomino is shown folded in (c) to form an open-top cubical box. Find which of the other pentominoes will form a net for the box and shade the square corresponding to its base.

77 The hexominoes

Which of the shapes in (a) could be folded to make a cube?

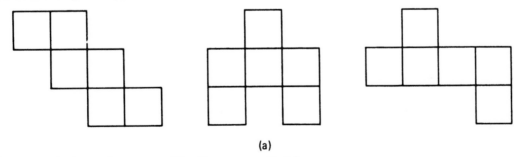

(a)

Shapes made from six squares like these are called *hexominoes*. There are 35 different hexominoes. Try to find them all – it may help if you use squared paper and do this with a partner. Record your results carefully so that you can quickly see if two are the same.

Eleven of the hexominoes can be folded to form a cube. When you have found a new hexomino see if you can decide whether or not it will form a cube before you fold it. Check by cutting out the shape and folding. How often were you wrong?

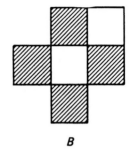

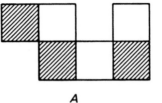

A   B

(b)

The two new hexominoes *A* and *B* shown in diagram (b) have had alternate squares shaded as in a chessboard pattern. Shape *A* will have three black squares while shape *B* will have either four black squares or two black squares. Because of this shape *A* is said to be *odd* and shape *B* is said to be *even*.

Shade all your hexominoes and decide which are *odd* and which *even*. How many *even* ones are there?

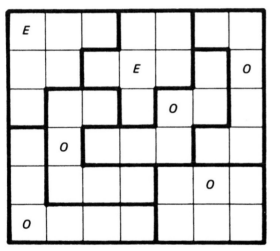

(c)

Diagram (c) shows one way of dissecting a 7 × 6 rectangle into seven hexominoes. In this example two of the hexominoes are *even* and five are *odd*.

Find other ways of dissecting a 7 × 6 rectangle into hexominoes and in each case note the numbers of *odd* and *even* ones.

Explain why it is impossible to dissect this rectangle into seven *even* hexominoes.

Is it possible to form a rectangle using all the 35 different hexominoes?

58

78 Building up cubes

For this activity you ideally need some interlocking cubes
such as Multilink or Centicube. It would be worth the effort
to obtain some for they are colourful, easy to handle, fit
together easily, but most of all they will stimulate you into
thinking creatively in three dimensions.

Make two shapes like the
one in (a) using four cubes.
You will be able to fit them
together to make a 2 x 2 x 2
cube as in (b).

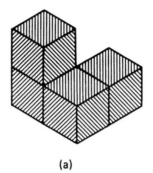

(a)

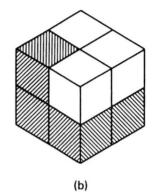

(b)

There are two other shapes which can be made with four
unit cubes which are also half a cube. Find them.

How many other ways could a 2 x 2 x 2 cube be constructed from two shapes where the shapes themselves are
formed from unit cubes?

The wide interest in shapes formed by fitting unit cubes
together has probably grown from the Soma Cube puzzle
invented by the Danish mathematician Piet Hein. It consists
of the seven shapes shown in (c). The object is to fit them
together to form a 3 x 3 x 3 cube.

  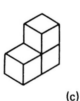

(c)

Make these shapes with your interlocking cubes and then
try to form the larger cube with them. There is more than
one solution. If you want to make a permanent set it is not
too difficult if you start by buying a length of wood with
a 2 cm x 2 cm cross-section, cutting it into suitable lengths,
and gluing together. The set is available commercially if you
prefer – either way the set will give you hours of amusement.

Why not be original however, and use the interlocking
unit cubes to design an interesting set of shapes to make up
a 3 x 3 x 3 cube and challenge your friends with it.

See how many different shapes you can make using five
unit cubes which are essentially different from the twelve
pentominoes.

79 Half a cube

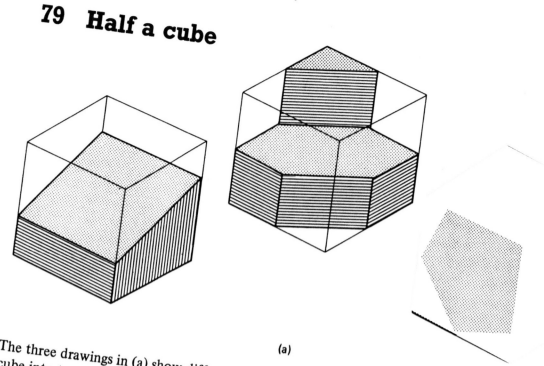

(a)

The three drawings in (a) show different ways to divide a
cube into two identical halves. Try to find other ways of
doing this and then make models of them using card.
In Activity 78 you will have found ways of using unit
cubes to build up a larger cube. A modification of this
method could help you to find interesting ways of dividing
a cube into two. Three more ways are shown in (b).

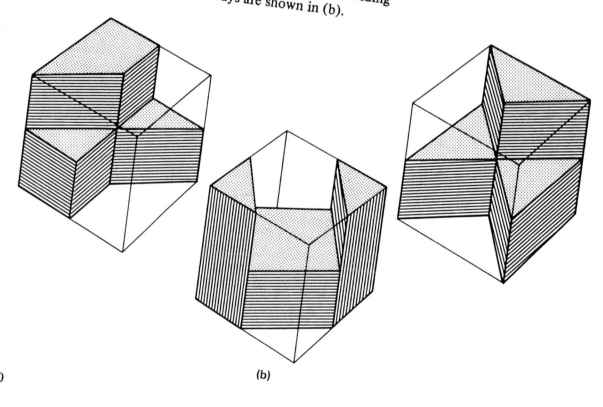

(b)

80 Make yourself a polyhedron construction kit

Draw an equilateral triangle and a square, each with a side of 4 cm, accurately on a piece of card. Next draw in the tabs $\frac{1}{2}$ cm wide as shown in (a), taking care with the indentations at each end. Cut these shapes out carefully as you will need them as templates to mark out further identical shapes.

To start with cut out eight triangle shapes and six square shapes. Score the edges *AB, BC, CA, PQ*, etc. so that the tabs fold easily.

You now need some elastic bands. Place the edge of one shape next to the edge of another shape and pinch the tabs together, having first folded them up. Now fasten them together by stretching an elastic band around them (see (b)).

Using this technique you can now fit further shapes edge to edge until you have a solid shape. With the triangles and squares already cut out you can make up a tetrahedron, a cube, an octahedron, a triangular prism and many other shapes. Some of these are shown in (c) without the tabs drawn in, but the invisible edges drawn with a dotted line.

Most of the shapes drawn here are straightforward except possibly the square anti-prism. This shape can be pictured as one square above another square turned at 45° to it and linked by a ring of eight triangles – a triangle joins the edge of one square to the vertex of the other.

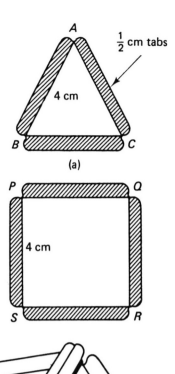

(a)

(b)

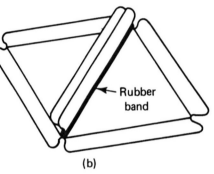

Rubber band

(c)

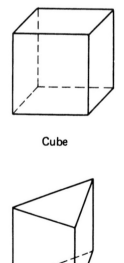

Cube

Octahedron

Tetrahedron

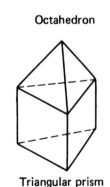

Triangular prism

Triangular prism joined to tetrahedron

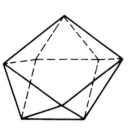

Square anti-prism

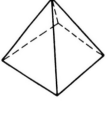

Square-based pyramid

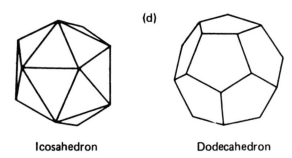

(d)

Icosahedron   Dodecahedron

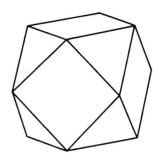

Cuboctahedron

To create larger and more elaborate polyhedra you will
need to make more triangles and squares and other shapes.

To make the beautifully symmetric icosahedron which
has five triangles meeting at every vertex, you will need
twenty triangle shapes, while the dodecahedron requires
twelve new regular pentagon shapes (see (d)).

Some more polyhedra to make are shown in (e). These
require only squares and triangles but should you wish
to incorporate pentagons and hexagons you will need to
ensure that they have the same length edge, that is 4 cm.
The best way to construct any regular polygon is to divide
a circle into the same number of sectors as the polygon is
to have sides. First though the radius of the circle must be
right or the polygon will end up with the wrong length of
edge. The details for the hexagon and pentagon are shown
in (f). Why is the radius 4 cm for the hexagon and not for
the pentagon?

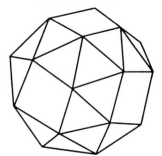

Snub cube

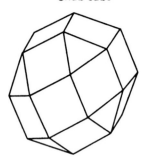

Rhombicuboctahedron

(e)

(f)

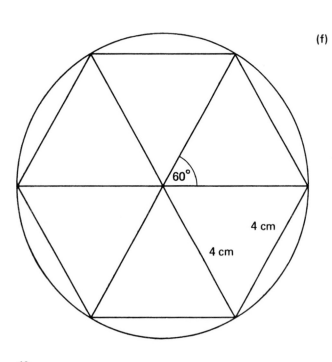

60°

4 cm

4 cm

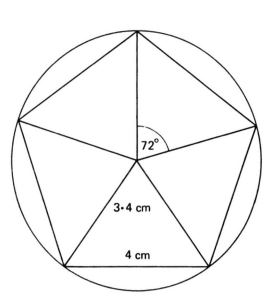

72°

3·4 cm

4 cm

The advantage of this construction kit is that you can easily dismantle a polyhedron and use the shapes to make another. Should you wish to make a model more permanent however, you could staple the tabs together. Cutting out the shapes can be tedious but creating new polyhedra is fun!

When you have cut out twelve pentagonal shapes to make the dodecahedron then you can try to make the rhombicosidodecahedron shown in (g). It is very impressive when complete and looks particularly fine if it is in three colours, one colour for each shape.

To make it you require twelve pentagons, twenty triangles and thirty squares. When you look at your finished model you will see that the pentagons are in the same relative positions as in a dodecahedron and the triangles are in the same relative positions as in an icosahedron. You can also see that at every vertex there is a pentagon next to a square which is next to a triangle and finally a second square.

If you want to find more about polyhedra there are many attractive books on the subject but one of the best is still *Mathematical Models* by Cundy and Rollett, which was first published in 1951 by Oxford University Press.

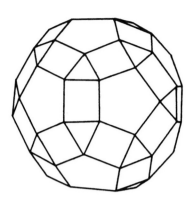

(g)   Rhombicosidodecahedron

81 The dodecahedron and stellated dodecahedron

The dodecahedron is one of the five regular solids known as the Platonic solids. The other four are the tetrahedron, the cube, the octahedron and the icosahedron.

In each of these the faces are identical regular polygons and each vertex looks the same as any other. The dodecahedron has twelve faces which are each regular pentagons – an enterprising manufacturer has produced a plastic version with a calendar month on each face.

It is a good model to make for not only is it a satisfying shape in its own right, but it can also be used as a base to make the very attractive stellated version. The construction which follows is for half the net of a dodecahedron. When this one has been drawn either on paper or card further copies can easily be produced by placing your drawing over a piece of card and using a compass point pricking through at all the vertices (corners) of the net.

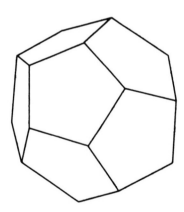

Dodecahedron

(i) Draw a large circle.

(ii) Draw five lines from the centre, O, to the circumference of the circle at $72°$ to each other, OA, OB, OC, OD, OE.

(iii) Join AB, BC, CD, DE and EA to form a regular pentagon.

(iv) Draw in all the diagonals of $ABCDE$. These diagonals form a smaller pentagon $PQRST$ in the centre. This pentagon will form a face of the dodecahedron so make its edges stand out using a biro.

(v) Now draw in the diagonals of $PQRST$ (shown dotted) and extend them to form the edges of the outer ring of pentagons. Outline the edges of the ring of pentagons clearly.

(vi) Prick through onto card to form as many nets as required.

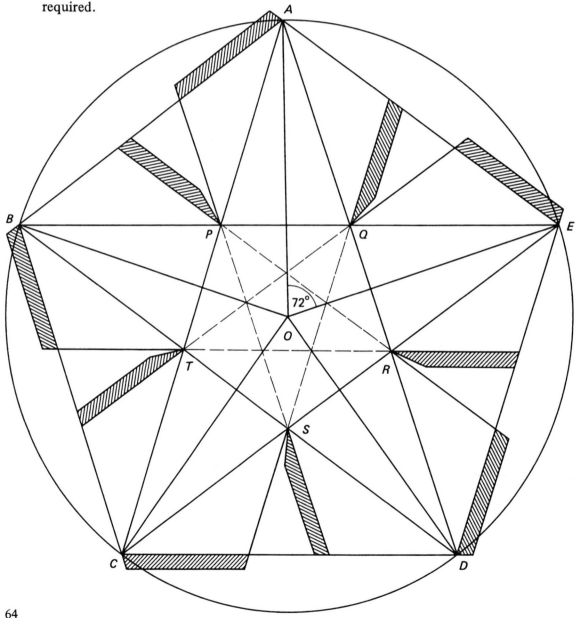

(vii) Draw in the additional nets and then add tabs to every
other edge as shown.
(viii) Cut out the nets and score along all lines which have
to be folded such as *PQ* and where a tab joins a face.
(ix) Use a quick drying glue such as UHU to stick your
nets together.

Do not be in too much of a hurry to finish. The first
stages need to be quite accurate or you will end up with a
net which doesn't fit together.

When you have successfully made the dodecahedron you
can stellate it to make an excellent Christmas decoration. It
is necessary to add points in the shape of five-sided pyramids
to each face of the dodecahedron.
The sides of these pyra-
mids are isosceles triangles
identical to *APQ* in the net
for the dodecahedron.

The net for a 'point' is easily
constructed by first drawing
a semi-circle with radius equal
to the diagonal of the pentagons which form the dodecahedron. Divide the semi-circle
into five equal sectors by
drawing radii at 36° intervals
as shown.

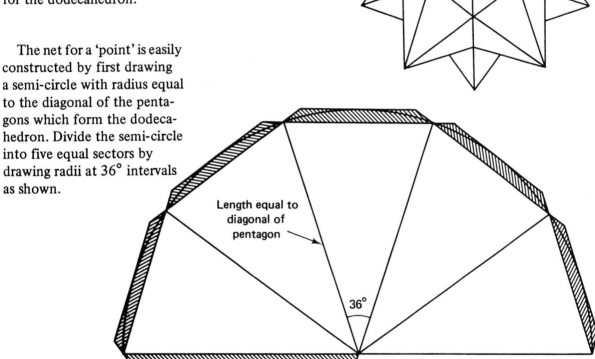

Length equal to
diagonal of
pentagon

36°

Add the tabs and score the fold lines. You will need
twelve identical nets so try folding your first one to see
if it fits together with your dodecahedron before copying
it.
When your model is complete you should see that the
faces of adjacent points all lie in planes to form pentagrams
(five-pointed stars).

82 An isometry game

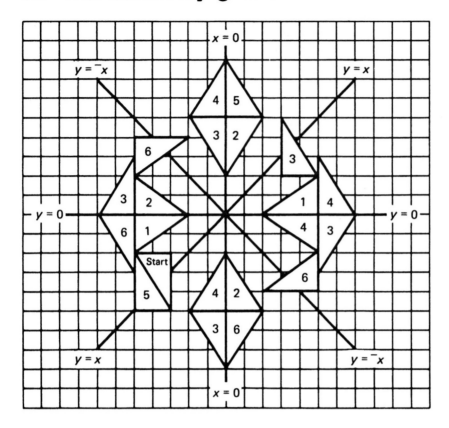

The piece

This game involves a knowledge of reflections, rotations, translations and their combinations. This set of transformations is known as the *isometries*, hence the name of the game.

Before you can play you will need to make:

(i) a board marked as above and a movable piece the same shape and size as the triangles on the board;

(ii) a pack of cards – see below.

The cards

Each card describes a transformation which the player who holds it can make to the movable triangle on the board. The cards are of two kinds:

(i) cards which give the exact details of a transformation such as

> *REFLECTION*   Mirror line: $y = x$

(ii) joker cards which give a player some freedom of choice in deciding the details of the transformation.

A suggested layout of the cards is shown here.

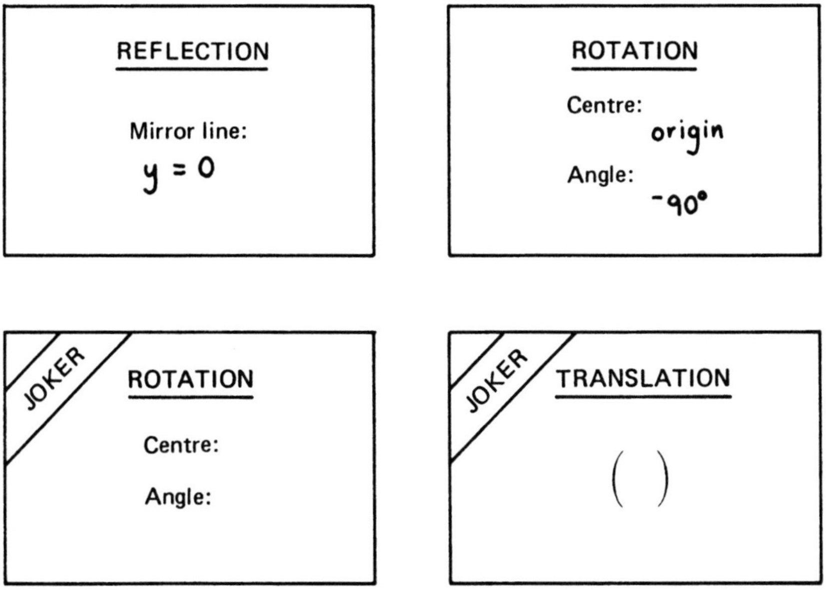

REFLECTION	ROTATION
Mirror line:	Centre: origin
$y = 0$	Angle: $^-90°$

JOKER ROTATION	JOKER TRANSLATION
Centre:	$(\ \ )$
Angle:	

There are 42 cards in the pack and they are made up as follows:

	Centre	Angle of rotation	Number of cards
ROTATIONS	Origin	$^+90°$	3
		$^-90°$	3
		$180°$	3
	The right-angle of the triangle	$^+90°$	2
		$^-90°$	2
		$180°$	2
REFLECTIONS		*Mirror line*	
		$x = 0$	3
		$y = 0$	3
		$y = x$	3
		$y = -x$	3
JOKERS	Translation		7
	Rotation:	centre angle	4
	Reflection:	equation of mirror line	4

Rules of play

The game can be played by two, three or four players.

(i) Deal five cards to each player, having first shuffled them, and place the remaining pack face-down on the table.

(ii) Decide, by throwing a dice or some other means, who plays first. The players then take turns to play.

(iii) When it is a player's turn he must attempt to move the triangular piece from where it was left by the previous player to another triangle on the board. The moves he is allowed correspond to the cards he holds in his hand at that time. The move can correspond to one card or a combination of cards. In the case of a combination the intermediate positions of the piece need not correspond to a marked triangle. The cards must be placed on a 'throw-away' pile face-up beside the unused pile in the order in which they are played.

(iv) When a player has made his move, he takes a card or cards from the top of the unused pack to top up the number of cards held in his hand to five.

(v) A player scores the number of points corresponding to the number marked on the triangle where he lands.

(vi) The *object of the game* is to score the most points, so clearly a running total will need to be kept for each player.

(vii) If a player cannot make a move or if he prefers not to move he may throw away one card and pick up a new one.

(viii) When using a joker card a player must announce the details (e.g. the equation of a mirror line) before moving the piece.

(ix) If a player believes that another player's move does not correspond to the card or cards used he may challenge it. If proved right, the triangle is returned to its former position and the player at fault misses his turn.

(x) The game ends when the pile of unused cards is empty and no-one can move. Alternatively play can be continued at this stage by shuffling the throw-away pile and turning it face down to be drawn from.

The game as it stands is fairly basic, and you can elaborate on it in a variety of ways, but even so you should enjoy challenging your friends and using combinations of transformations to move the triangle piece to obtain as high a score as possible.

83 Sawing up a cube

A 3 cm wooden cube is to be
sawn into 27 one-centimetre
cubes. Is it possible to achieve
this with fewer than six saw
cuts?

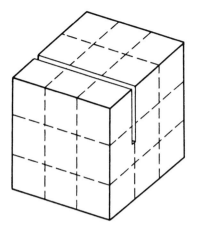

84 The improbable hole

Improbable though it may
seem, it is possible to cut a
hole through a solid cube so
that a cube, larger than the
original, can be passed in one
end and out the other.

How do you cut the hole?

85 Equilateral triangle to square

Construct an equilateral triangle ABC then divide it into the
four pieces shown where

$$AP = BP, \quad CQ = BQ, \quad AR = \tfrac{1}{4} AC, \quad CS = \tfrac{1}{4} CA$$

and PM and SN are at right angles to RQ. 8 cm is a good
length to use for AC.

Cut the pieces out of card (or for a more permanent puzzle
use plywood or hardboard) and then rearrange them to form
a 'square'.

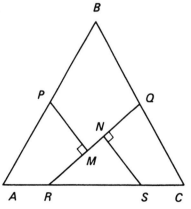

86 Squaring the urn

The cross-section of an urn is shown here shaded. It is composed of parts of four circles of the same size as indicated.

Show how, with two straight cuts, this shape can be divided into three pieces which can be rearranged to make a square.

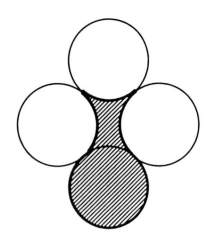

87 The baffled housewife

Mrs Smith often walked to the bus-stop on the main road to catch a bus into the shopping centre. She didn't ever bother with timetables because it was a busy route and she could catch either a P bus or a Q bus. She knew that there were six buses an hour of each kind so she never had long to wait. What did surprise her, however, was that she hardly ever seemed to travel on a Q bus. She decided to keep a regular check on the kind of bus she caught and found that she only travelled on a Q bus on one ride in ten.

She was baffled! Can you help her?

88 Invert the triangle

A triangle of pennies is made as in (a). What is the smallest number of pennies which have to be moved to turn the triangle pattern upside down as in (b)?

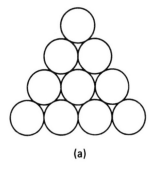

(a)

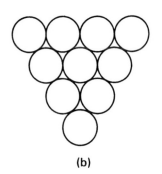

(b)

89 Knight's tours

One of the classical problems in recreational mathematics is to investigate paths on a chessboard which a knight can follow in such a way that it visits every square on the board once and only once. Many famous mathematicians such as De Moivre, Euler and Vandermonde have written about this problem over the last 200 years but there is always something new to be found.

One solution due to De Moivre for the 8 x 8 board is indicated in (a) where the squares are numbered to indicate the knight's progress. In (b) is shown an alternative way of representing the same path. They both have their merits and you can decide which is the more appropriate for your investigations. (You will need a plentiful supply of squared paper however if you are to make any progress whichever method you use.) The second method using lines to connect the squares has not been completed but it already shows the strategy of De Moivre's solution which was essentially to move round the board in one direction always keeping as close to the outer boundary as possible. Copy diagram (b) onto squared paper and complete De Moivre's solution before trying one of your own.

34	49	22	11	36	39	24	1
21	10	35	50	23	12	37	40
48	33	62	57	38	25	2	13
9	20	51	54	63	60	41	26
32	47	58	61	56	53	14	3
19	8	55	52	59	64	27	42
46	31	6	17	44	29	4	15
7	18	45	30	5	16	43	28

(a)

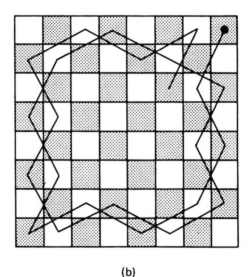

(b)

In a problem like this it is often helpful to start with a smaller board to get a feel for the way in which a knight can move to the other squares around it on a board.

On a 3 x 3 board it is soon clear that a knight's tour of the whole board is impossible. Either the knight starts on an outside square when it can easily visit all the outer squares but not the middle square, or it starts in the middle when no move is possible.

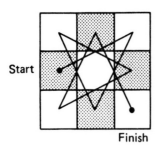

Start

Finish

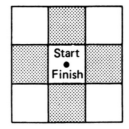

Start
•
Finish

(c)

Is it possible to find a knight's tour on a 4 x 4 board? Diagram (d) shows a false trail which ran out of moves after the fourth. If you cannot achieve all sixteen squares, what is the largest number which you can visit without retracing your steps?

Investigate paths on 5 x 5, 6 x 6 and 7 x 7 boards.

Diagram (e) shows a knight's tour on an 8 x 4 rectangular board.

Is it possible to find a knight's tour on a smaller rectangular board?

			2
	1		
		3	
4			

(d)

18	13	32	9	28	5	22	1
31	10	19	16	21	2	25	6
14	17	12	29	8	27	4	23
11	30	15	20	3	24	7	26

(e)

It is interesting to investigate other shapes which can be toured by a knight. The shape in diagram (f) can be, although the author had convinced himself it was not possible when he first investigated it!

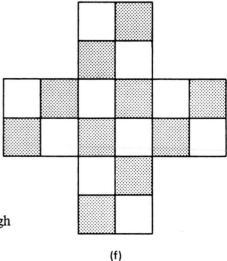

(f)

However, to return to the classical problem on a square board, the mathematicians who investigated it tried to find solutions with special properties. One type of solution was to find a knight's tour which ended a knight's move from the starting square. A solution of this type due to Euler is shown below. Such a solution is said to form a re-entrant path. The solution shown in (g) has a further intriguing property in that one half of the board is completed before the other half is entered.

58	43	60	37	52	41	62	35
49	46	57	42	61	36	53	40
44	59	48	51	38	55	34	63
47	50	45	56	33	64	39	54
22	7	32	1	24	13	18	15
31	2	23	6	19	16	27	12
8	21	4	29	10	25	14	17
3	30	9	20	5	28	11	26

(g) Euler's re-entrant half-board solution

1	48	31	50	33	16	63	18
30	51	46	3	62	19	14	35
47	2	49	32	15	34	17	64
52	29	4	45	20	61	36	13
5	44	25	56	9	40	21	60
28	53	8	41	24	57	12	37
43	6	55	26	39	10	59	22
54	27	42	7	58	23	38	11

(h) Euler's magic square solution

Try to find a re-entrant path on a 6 × 6 board.

There is a neat proof to show that a re-entrant path on any board having an odd number of squares is impossible. See if you can find the reason.

Re-entrant paths are possible on a variety of shapes. Try this one (i).

Another clever solution due to Euler which defeated many other seekers was that of a knight's tour whose squares when numbered in the usual fashion formed an 8 × 8 magic square (i.e. the sums of the numbers in any row or column, but not diagonal, add up to the same total, in this case 260). This square is given in (h). Check its 'magic' property and investigate the symmetry of its path.

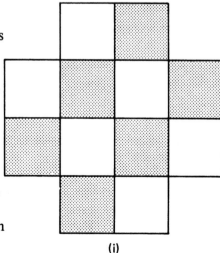

(i)

An interesting game of strategy for two players based on a knight's tour can be played as follows. Start on any square of a 5 × 5 board and produce a knight's path by players taking in turn to make a knight's move from the last position reached. The move must not land on a square previously used and the winner is the last player able to move.

90 Distance has a new meaning

If you are a chess player you will be aware that the ease with which a knight can reach a particular square is not very closely related to its physical distance away. The knight's peculiar leap-frog step which takes it from a square of one colour to a square of another colour makes a nonsense of our commonsense ideas about distance.

Suppose a knight is on a black square and a pawn is on a white square next to it, then it will take a minimum of three moves on the knight's part to capture the pawn. So, in this sense, the adjacent white square is a distance of three moves from the black square. This is shown in diagram (a). In (b) is shown the reason why an adjacent black square would only be considered to be a distance of two moves away.

Diagram (c) shows all the squares that a knight can reach from a white square in two moves. As they are all the same distance from the knight they correspond to a knight's circle! Why are they all white squares?

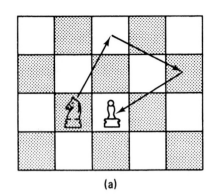

(a)

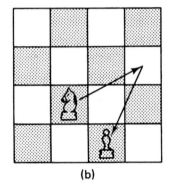

(b)

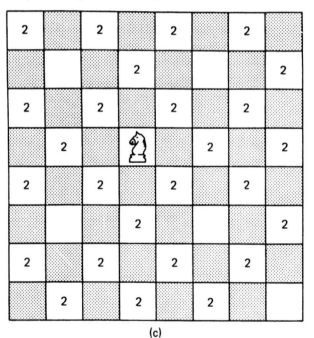

(c)

What distance are all the other unmarked white squares from the knight?

Take a piece of 8 x 8 square paper representing a chessboard and imagine a knight at one corner in a white square. Now mark all the squares on the board to show their knight's distance from the corner. How far is the opposite corner?

74

91 Avoid that snooker

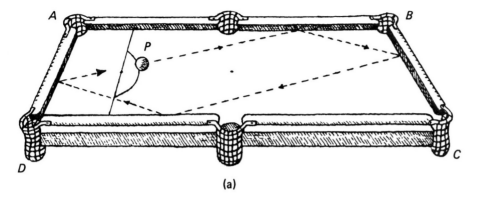

(a)

When a ball P is struck by a cue towards the side cushion of a snooker table it bounces off as if the cushion is a mirror. A typical path of a ball which is first hit towards the side cushion AB is shown in diagram (a). Always supposing there is no ball in its path the ball will then be 'reflected' off the end cushion BC followed by the side cushion CD etc. as shown until it comes to rest.

In the game of snooker the problem is often to strike the cue ball P to make contact with a particular coloured ball which has been purposely snookered (hidden) behind other balls by one's opponent. If any other ball is hit then points are lost so the skill of the game is to learn how to use the side walls of the table to bounce the cue ball onto the target ball.

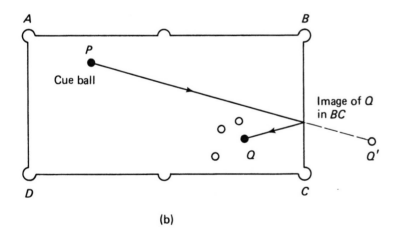

(b)

Diagram (b) represents a situation where Q, the target ball, is snookered by three other balls. In this case the cue ball can be bounced off the end cushion BC. To decide where the cue ball must strike BC, mark in Q' the mirror image of Q in BC, and hit the cue ball towards Q'. The cue ball will then automatically 'reflect' off BC towards Q.

This method can be neatly extended to get out of trickier situations (at least in theory!) where the ball is bounced off two or more cushions. Diagram (c) shows how the cue ball çan be struck to bounce off AB, then off BC before hitting the target ball T.

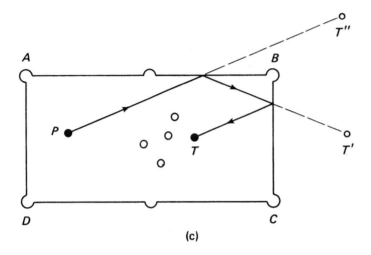

(c)

Because the cue ball is to bounce off BC towards T, it must travel towards BC in the direction of T', where T' is the mirror image of T in BC. To do this it must travel towards AB in the direction of T'', where T'' is the mirror image of T' in AB.

Find where to hit the cue ball P to make contact with the target ball T in the following situations.

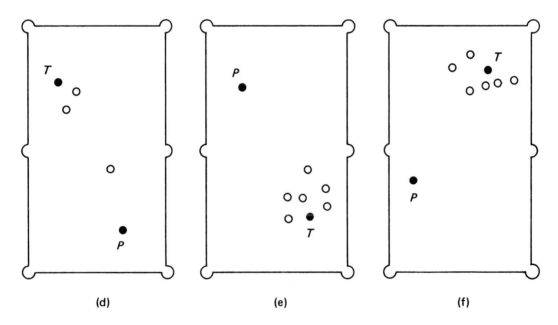

(d)   (e)   (f)

92 Euler's relation

Euler discovered a simple relation connecting the numbers
of vertices, edges and faces of polyhedra which has come to
be seen as an important theorem in the new branch of mathematics known as graph theory. Complete the table.

Polyhedron		Vertices (V)	Edges (E)	Faces (F)	V − E + F
	Cube				
	Tetrahedron				
	Pyramid				
	Triangular prism				
	Octahedron				
	Hexagonal prism				

You should now be in a position to state Euler's relation for yourself.

Check your guess by seeing if the relation is satisfied on other polyhedra.

Euler only saw his relation as a property of polyhedra, but later mathematicians realised that the relation is really about networks on a surface of a sphere or in a plane.

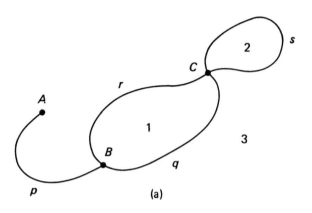

(a)

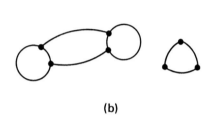

(b)

Consider the network in (a). It has *three* nodes A, B, C; *four* arcs p, q, r, s; and it divides the surface into *three* regions 1, 2, 3. These numbers satisfy the relation

$$N - A + R = 2$$

where N is the number of nodes, A the number of arcs, and R the number of regions. Do you see any similarity with your relation for polyhedra?

Now test the relation above for other networks.

Did you try any networks which were not connected such as the one in (b)?

You will find that the relation above will need to be modified depending on the number of separate parts to the network. See if you can find a formula which will be true no matter how many parts there are in the network.

The relation between Euler's relation and the network relation can be seen in the following way:

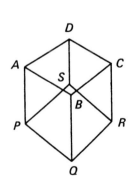

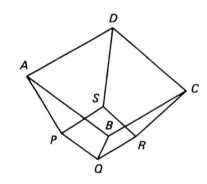

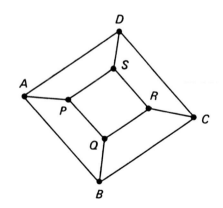

Imagine a cube made of an elastic material which can be stretched as shown and then flattened into a network in a plane. Each vertex of the original cube is now a node in the network. Each edge of the original cube is now an arc in the network.

Each face of the cube is now a region in the plane except for plane *ABCD*, but this can be replaced by the region outside the network.

This kind of transformation can be carried out on all the polyhedra considered with similar results but, be warned, polyhedra with holes need more thought.

Euler's relation can be generalised even more by looking at the ways in which three-dimensional space can be divided into different regions.

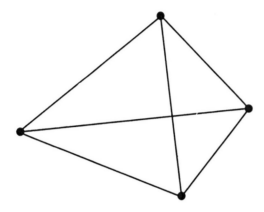

Consider the tetrahedron which is the simplest polyhedron. It divides space into two regions and

$$V - E + F - R = 4 - 6 + 4 - 2 = 0$$

where R is the number of regions. Now look at the cube fastened to a pyramid. This compound divides space into three regions. There are: nine vertices, sixteen edges and ten faces.

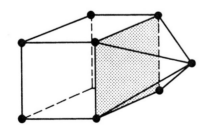

Here again

$$V - E + F - R = 0$$

which suggests another relation springing from Euler's original one. Try it out on other ways of dividing up space.

93 Curves from intersecting circles

Many interesting curves and patterns can be found by drawing sets of intersecting circles. Two of these are shown here to give you a start.

In the first example two sets of circles are drawn from two centres A and B. Here the original drawing was made with the distance $AB = 12$ cm and the circles increasing in radius by 1 cm at a time. A set of circles all drawn with the same centre and looking like the ripples formed when a pebble is dropped into a pool are called concentric. When two concentric sets of circles are drawn as below with the circles equally spaced then their intersections lie on sets of ellipses. Four of the ellipses have been drawn in. The ringed numbers give a clue to why the ellipses are formed. For the ellipse labelled 20 you will find that for every point P on it $AP + BP = 20$.

This is easily checked. Take, for example, the point which is on the eighth circle from A and you will find that it is on the twelfth circle from B.

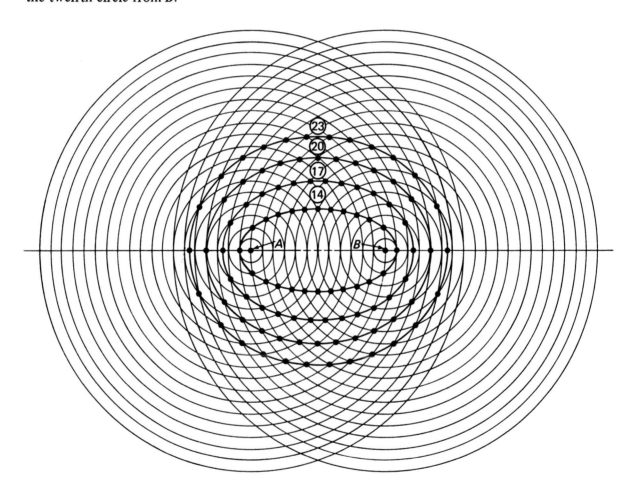

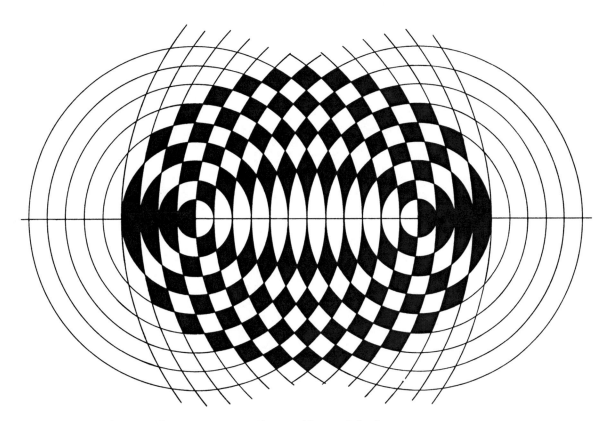

Try marking in the ellipses corresponding to 18 and 26. If you have access to a photocopier then it is a good idea to draw two sets of intersecting concentric circles and make several copies of them before marking in the ellipses. Above can be seen the way in which shading in the alternate regions in a chessboard fashion can also highlight the ellipses and make an attractive pattern into the bargain.

Can you see another family of curves in this diagram?

The second example is shown on the right. The curve which appears as the boundary of all the circles is known as a *cardioid*.

To produce this diagram start with a base circle and mark a point A on it. All the other circles are formed by taking different points on the circumference of the circle and adjusting the radius so that the circles go through A.

Draw as many circles as you want to get the boundary clearly.

What will happen if you start with the point A not on the circumference of the base circle?

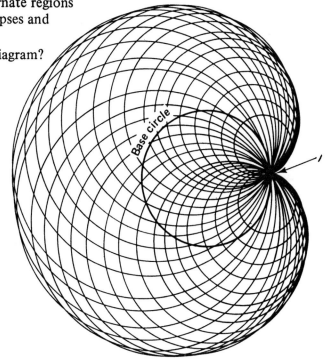

94 Make yourself a ruled surface

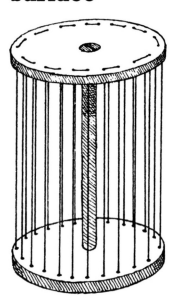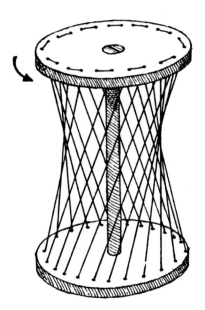

Take two discs of plywood, hardboard or thick card about 8 cm in diameter and drill 24 small holes equally spread around the circumference. Metal lids could also be used from old paint tins for example, although you could buy the plywood bases used in cane work from a craft shop. Now screw the discs through their centres to the ends of a piece of dowel about 15 cm long. Thread shirring elastic through the discs so that the elastic is parallel to the dowel as shown in the left-hand diagram above. The effect is that of a circular cylinder.

Now hold the bottom disc and turn the top disc. The effect will be to pull the shirring elastic at an angle and the lines they form will appear to all lie on a curved surface known as a *hyperboloid*.

This surface is called a ruled surface because of the way the straight lines lie in it. Contrast this with the surface of a sphere for example on which straight lines are impossible.

You will probably recognise the surface as that of the giant cooling towers seen at some electricity power stations. It is also the shape which a soap film takes up when it forms between two wire rings.

95 Squares

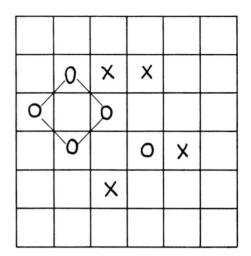

This is another version of noughts and crosses which can be played on squared paper. Mark off a board which is a 6 × 6 square or larger.

Players mark noughts and crosses alternately and the winner is the first player to make four of his marks at the vertices of a square. In the game shown the player marking noughts has won.

How many ways of making a square on a 6 × 6 board are there?

Another version of the game is to play until the board has been filled with marks and then assess which player has the larger number of squares.

Yet another alternative is to play to avoid making squares. The loser is then the first player to form a square.

96 The hungry bookworm

A bookworm started eating its way through a five-volume set of encyclopaedias starting at the front cover of volume I and ate its way through to the outside of the back cover of volume V. If each volume was 3 cm thick how far had the bookworm travelled? (You may assume the volumes are stacked in numerical order.)

97 Place the motorway junction

Building roads can be very expensive so civil engineers try to make them as short as possible. The line of a new motorway as it passes by the small towns of Green Glades and Pleasant Pastures is to be as straight as a ruler. It is proposed to make one junction on the motorway for the local inhabitants and join it to the towns by straight roads as shown. Where should the junction be positioned to minimise the total length of the road G to J to P?

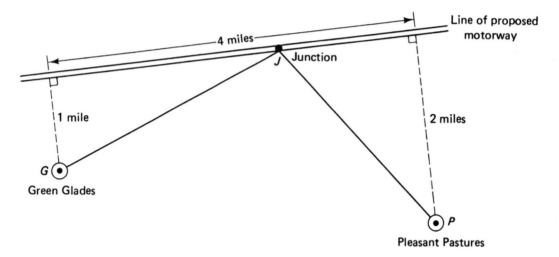

98 How fast can you cycle?

In a time trial a cyclist wanted to average 40 km per hour between two towns A and C which are 10 kilometres apart. A village B is sited exactly halfway between A and C and is reached after a long climb up from A. When the cyclist had climbed up to B he calculated that his average speed so far was only 20 km per hour. How fast must he ride on the descent from B to C if he is to attain the overall average speed of 40 km per hour?

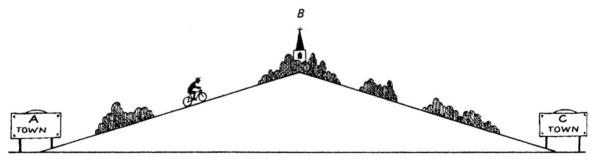

99 The bob-sleigh run

It is proposed to design a new bob-sleigh run at a well-known ski resort. The run is to start at the summit of a hill, S, near the ski lift and end 500 m lower in the village V. No expense is to be spared to build the run to make the descent as fast as possible. What line should the path take from S to V to achieve this?

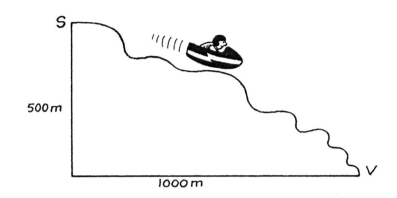

100 Know your vowels!

This table contains each of the five vowels – A, E, I, O, U – five times, Show how to cut the 5 x 5 square into five different pieces each of which contains all the vowels once only.

When you have solved this one try making a similar one for yourself.

E	A	I	O	I
U	E	U	E	O
O	I	A	O	A
I	U	E	A	I
A	O	U	E	U

101 Space filling

A unit cube can be fitted together with seven other identical cubes to make a larger cube with an edge of 2 units. How many unit cubes are needed to make a cube with an edge of 3 units?

Given a supply of identical regular tetrahedra (i.e. triangular pyramids whose faces are all equilateral triangles) can you fit them together to make a larger tetrahedron, and if so how many would you need?

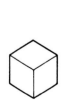
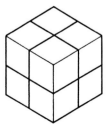

102 Diagonals of a rectangle

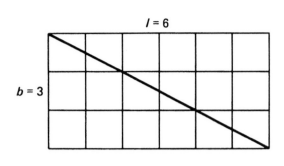

$l = 6$

$b = 3$

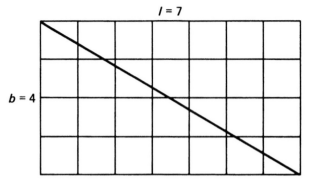

$l = 7$

$b = 4$

You will need some squared paper for this activity.

Mark out different size rectangles on the squared paper where the length (l) and the breadth (b) is a whole number of squares. Now draw in a diagonal of each rectangle and note the number of squares which it crosses, d. Make a table as here:

l	b	d
6	3	6
7	4	10

There is a nice relationship connecting l, b and d. See if you can find it.

You may need several examples before you spot the connection but it is not difficult.

103 Straight lines divide a plane

The diagram shows how three straight lines drawn in a plane can divide it into at most seven regions.

Complete the following table showing the maximum number of regions which can be formed in each case.

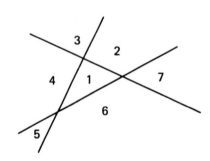

No. of lines (n)	0	1	2	3	4	5	6	7
No. of regions (r)				7				

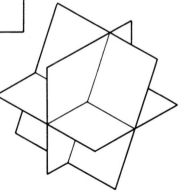

By continuing the sequence without drawing lines can you tell how many regions can be formed with (i) 10 lines, (ii) 100 lines?

If you think this was easy try yourself out on finding the maximum number of regions which three-dimensional space can be divided into by intersecting planes!

104 Number sequences - differencing

The last activity and some later ones will involve forming a sequence of numbers and then trying to detect the underlying pattern so that it can be continued indefinitely. One technique which can help in many situations is to look at the difference between the numbers of the sequence and their next door neighbour. In the following sequence it is not at all obvious what the next term would be until you form the differences:

Sequence	3		8		15		24		35
Differences		5		7		9		11	

It is clear now that, with the evidence available, the next difference is likely to be 13 and then the sixth term in the sequence would be 48.

What is the tenth term in this sequence?

Find the next term in each of the following sequences by using this difference method:

(i)	3	5	9	15	23
(ii)	3	8	18	33	53
(iii)	2	3	8	17	30
(iv)	4	6	10	18	34

In each of the above the sequence of numbers formed from finding the differences was easy to continue so that the original sequence could soon be determined. The original sequence however may have led to a sequence of differences which was not obvious and then the differences of the differences can be found as in the following example.

Sequence	3		7		12		19		29		43
First differences		4		5		7		10		14	
Second differences		1		2		3		4			

What are the next two terms in the original sequence?

You should have noticed that the new sequence of numbers formed by differencing is one less at each stage so that you will require more terms of the original sequence to determine the pattern the more complicated it becomes.

87

Find the next term in each of the following sequences, taking differences as often as you require to determine the pattern:

(v)	0	2	5	11	22	40	
(vi)	0	1	4	12	28	55	
(vii)	0	1	3	10	28	65	131
(viii)	0	2	7	17	36	72	141

Make up some sequences yourself by starting with an easy one and using it as a sequence of differences. For example, if you take

$$1 \quad 2 \quad 3 \quad 4 \quad 5$$

as the starting sequence and choose 8 as the first term of the sequence for which this will be the differences then you will generate

	1		2		3		4		5	
8		9		11		14		18		23

This sequence could then be taken as the differences for a sequence starting with 3, say:

3 11 20 31 45 63 86

In this way you can make them as complex as you like. Work with a friend and interchange your sequences for the other to unravel.

105 Number patterns from dotty patterns

For this activity you will need either some dotty paper, a pinboard or a pegboard.

Diagram (a) shows the first three squares of a sequence starting from the one in the middle and growing outwards from the central dot.

From this sequence two number sequences can be constructed by counting
(i) the number of dots on the perimeter of each square,
(ii) the number of dots inside each square.

What is the tenth number in each sequence?

How about the hundredth number?

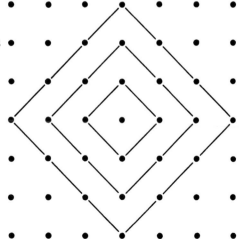

(a)

Another sequence known as the triangle numbers is formed by making a sequence of right-angled triangles as shown in diagram (b), and counting the number of dots inside each triangle:

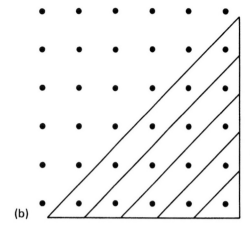

     1   3   6   10   ...

How many dots would there be inside the tenth triangle?

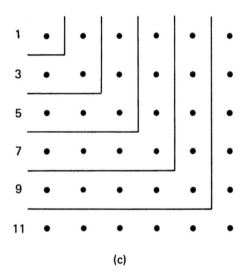

(b)

Diagram (c) shows how a square of dots can be divided up into a sequence of odd numbers so giving the pattern:

1	$= 1^2$
1 + 3	$= 2^2$
1 + 3 + 5	$= 3^2$
1 + 3 + 5 + 7	$= 4^2$
1 + 3 + 5 + 7 + 9	$= 5^2$
1 + 3 + 5 + 7 + 9 + 11	$= 6^2$

What is the sum of the first ten odd numbers?
Find the sum of the odd numbers

    1   3   5   7   ...   39

What is the sum of the odd numbers between 60 and 100?

(c)

106 Squares on a pinboard

How many different sizes of squares can you make on pinboards sized 2 x 2, 3 x 3, 4 x 4, ..., 8 x 8? Record your results.

   Write down the areas of the squares which can be made on an 8 x 8 pinboard in increasing order of size.

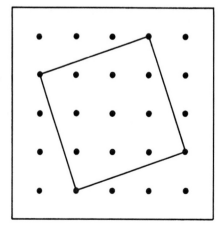

107 From polygons to frieze patterns

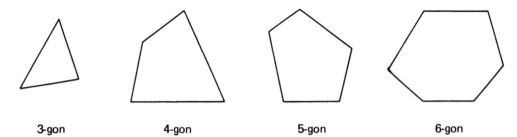

3-gon   4-gon   5-gon   6-gon

(i)   What are the special names we give the above polygons? Can you give the names of any polygons with more sides?

(ii)   How many diagonals can be drawn from one vertex (corner) of a polygon with 20 sides?

(iii) How many diagonals are there for a polygon with (a) 4 sides, (b) 5 sides, (c) 6 sides, . . . n sides?

(iv) What is the largest number of diagonals you can draw in (a) a 5-gon, (b) a 6-gon, (c) a 7-gon without the diagonals crossing?

Triangulation, the process of dividing a polygon into a number of triangles, is the basis of an important surveying technique but here we are more interested in the different ways a polygon can be triangulated and how to record the results.

The polygon $ABCDEF$ in diagram (a) has been triangulated by drawing in the three diagonals AC, AD and DF. Find two other distinctly different ways in which three diagonals could have been drawn to triangulate the same polygon.

The 7-gon in diagram (b) has been triangulated by four diagonals. How many other distinct ways can you find?

A neat way of recording the different triangulations is to number each vertex by the number of triangles which meet there. The triangulation of the polygon shown here could then be recorded as

$$1 \quad 4 \quad 1 \quad 3 \quad 1 \quad 3 \quad 2$$

Although which vertex you start at and whether you go clockwise or anti-clockwise would give a different number, the same digits would occur in the same sequence.

$$1 + 4 + 1 + 3 + 1 + 3 + 2 = 15$$

Would a different triangulation of a 7-gon lead to the same digit sum?

Explain your result.

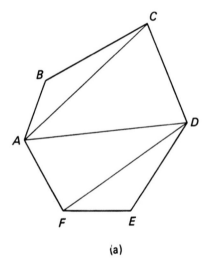

(a)

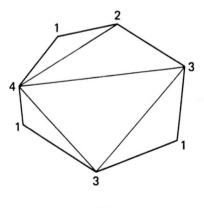

(b)

Take polygons with different numbers of sides and record the distinct ways of triangulating them as suggested above, or otherwise. Are you able to predict, without drawing, how many distinct ways a 10-sided polygon can be triangulated?

Frieze patterns

The sequences of numbers formed by triangulating polygons can be used to make some fascinating number patterns.

1		1		1		1		1		1		1		1		1		1		1		1		1		1		1
	1		4		1		3		1		3		2		1		4		1		3		1		3		2	
		3		3		2		2		2		5		1		3		3		2		2		2		5		
			2		5		1		3		3		2		2		2		5		1		3		3			
				3		2		1		4		1		3		1		3		2		1		4				
					1		1		1		1		1		1		1		1		1		1					

The first line is just a sequence of 1 s.

The second line is a sequence formed by the numbers generated when triangulating a polygon.

The third line is formed in the following way:

r	row 1
$p \quad q$	row 2
s	row 3

Form the product pq of two next door neighbours in row 2. Subtract 1 to get $(pq - 1)$. Obtain the number s to go in the third row between p and q by dividing $pq - 1$ by r, the number in row 1 above it:

$$s = \frac{pq - 1}{r}$$

The numbers in all the other lines are obtained using the same rule on the two previous rows. For example:

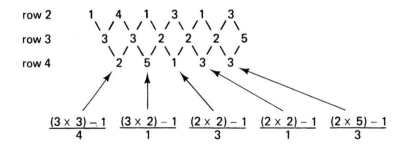

91

Try making some of these number patterns for yourself.
The greater the number of sides you have in the polygon
which you triangulate to obtain the sequence of numbers for
the second line, the broader will be your frieze. Here is
another example:

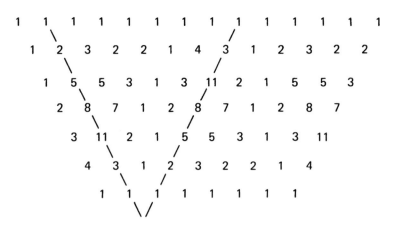

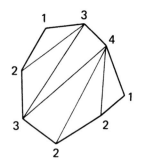

Note the diagonal patterns as well as the horizontal ones.
Frieze patterns are a new relatively unexplored field. See
what you can find out for yourself.

108 Games on a pegboard for one to play

A piece of pegboard (hardboard with holes in) and some
coloured pegs is all you need to spend hours happily playing
the following solitaire games. Alternatively you could use
counters or pawns on a chessboard.

Leapfrog

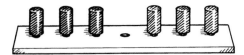

The first game requires a line of seven holes, three pegs of
one colour (say black) and three pegs of a second colour (say
red). Place them as shown with an empty hole between them.
A move consists of (i) moving a peg into the next position if
the hole is empty, or (ii) jumping over one piece to an empty
hole beyond like a capturing move in draughts.
    The two kinds of move are illustrated on the next page and
follow in turn from the starting position.

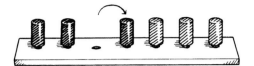 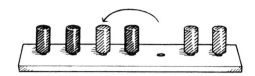

The object of the game is to find the smallest number of moves to interchange the black pegs and the red pegs.

Vary the game by having different numbers of pegs at each end and see if you can find a formula for the number of moves required for x black pegs and y red pegs to change ends.

All change!

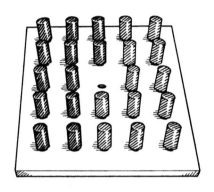

The second game is very similar to the first game but played on a square board. A 5 × 5 board is shown here with the starting position. There are twelve black pegs, twelve red pegs and an empty hole in the middle.

Moves are as in 'Leapfrog' but now the pegs can be moved from left to right or up and down. No diagonal moves are allowed.

Show how to interchange the two sets of pegs in 48 moves.

Solitaire

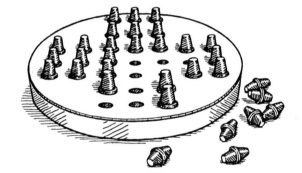

The third game has a very long history and is played across the world. It is available in a commercial form from cheap plastic versions to expensive ones in wood with coloured marbles for the pieces. However pegboard and coloured pegs make a suitable alternative.

In this game the board has 33 holes arranged in a cross as shown here. There are 32 pegs all of the same colour and they are initially arranged as shown leaving the central hole empty.

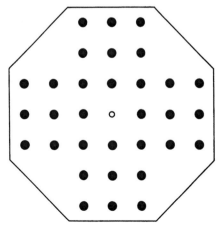

This time the only allowable move is to jump over an adjacent peg to an empty hole beyond. The peg which has been jumped over is removed from the board. Only across and up and down moves are allowed and the object is to remove all but one of the pegs.

There are many solutions but the best are considered to be those which end with the last peg in the centre.

Have a go!

There are several traditional problems on a solitaire board where the player has to try to end with a peg in the centre. Here are three of them.

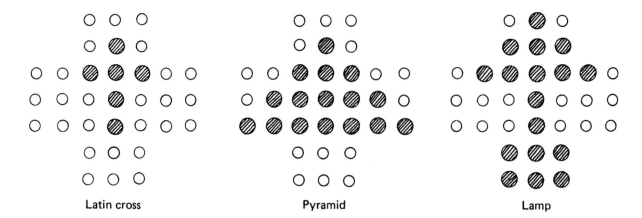

Latin cross   Pyramid   Lamp

109 Two of a kind

Shapes P and Q can each be divided into two identical pieces. They have been designed on the same principle so that when you have found the solution to one shape the other's solution should soon follow.

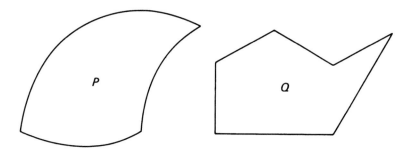

110 Colouring a cube

What is the smallest number of colours needed to paint a cube so that no two adjacent faces are the same?

How many distinctly different cubes can be obtained if four colours are used?

(A face can only be one colour and adjacent faces must be different colours.)

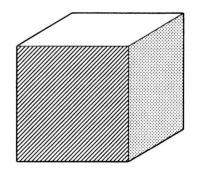

111 Cutting up a circle

This sequence of diagrams shows what happens when a
number of points are taken on the circumference of a circle
and all the chords joining the points are drawn in. If you
took a pair of scissors and cut along all the lines in each case
the circle will be cut into 2, 4, 8, 16 pieces.

How many pieces will the circle end up as if you do the
same with six points on the circumference?

Do not jump to conclusions!

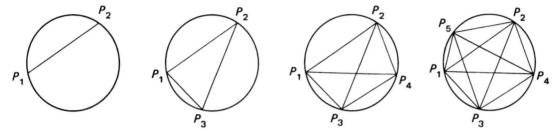

112 Square relations

The number 24 has the property that it is one short of a
square number, and its double is also one short of a square
number.

$$24 + 1 = 25 = 5^2$$
$$(24 \times 2) + 1 = 49 = 7^2$$

What is the next number with the same property?

113 The numerate gardener

A gardener had a number of equal square paving slabs which
he arranged to form two larger square patios of about the
same size as each other. Being a dab-hand with figures he
realised that with the same number of paving slabs he could
have produced two square patios but this time with one
much larger than the other. How many paving slabs did the
gardener have?

114 Magic triangles

The numbers 1, 2, 3, 4, 5, 6 have been arranged in a triangle so that the sum of the numbers along each side is always the same, 10. Show that the same numbers can be put on the triangle in a different way so that the totals along each side are still constant but equal to another number. There are three possibilities apart from the one shown. Numbers arranged to form a triangle like this are called magic.

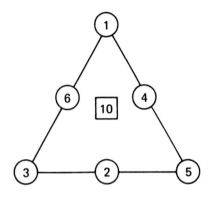

Now try arranging the following sets of numbers to form magic triangles:

      (i) 1 2 3 5 6 7
     (ii) 1 2 3 4 6 7

There are two different arrangements in each case.

115 Number patterns

There are many fascinating number patterns to investigate. Here are a few to start you thinking.

1 Choose a digit. Suppose you choose 5. Multiply 5 by 9 to obtain 45. Now work out

      $12\,345\,679 \times 45$

Are you surprised at the answer?
   Try another digit such as 3, multiply 3 by 9 to obtain 27 and then work out

      $12\,345\,679 \times 27$

Can you explain the answer?

2 This is similar to the above. Choose a digit, for example 2, multiply 2 by 7 to obtain 14, then work out

      $15\,873 \times 14$

Investigate other digits and explain the results.

3 Complete the following and explain the pattern.

      $143 \times 2 \times 7 =$
      $143 \times 3 \times 7 =$
      $143 \times 4 \times 7 =$
      $143 \times 5 \times 7 =$
      $143 \times 6 \times 7 =$
      $143 \times 7 \times 7 =$
      $143 \times 8 \times 7 =$
      $143 \times 9 \times 7 =$

4 Can you explain the patterns which emerge from the following calculations?

(i)
$$(0 \times 9) + 1 =$$
$$(1 \times 9) + 2 =$$
$$(12 \times 9) + 3 =$$
$$(123 \times 9) + 4 =$$
$$(1234 \times 9) + 5 =$$
. . .

(ii)
$$6 \times 7 =$$
$$66 \times 67 =$$
$$666 \times 667 =$$
$$6666 \times 6667 =$$
$$66666 \times 66667 =$$
. . .

116 Surprising subtractions

Choose any four digits such as 3, 6, 2, 8 and rearrange them to form the largest and smallest numbers possible, namely 8632 and 2368.

Subtract the smaller number from the larger number and repeat the process using the four digits in the answer as the new starting point:

$$\begin{array}{r} 8632 \\ -\ 2368 \\ \hline 6264 \end{array} \qquad \begin{array}{r} 6642 \\ -\ 2466 \\ \hline 4176 \end{array} \qquad \begin{array}{r} 7641 \\ -\ 1467 \\ \hline 6174 \end{array}$$

In this example the digits 1, 4, 6, 7 occur in the answer at the second stage and no new numbers are generated from then on.

Investigate what happens with different sets of four digits as a starting point and continue subtracting until no new numbers occur. What do you notice?

What is the longest chain of subtractions you can find before nothing new occurs?

117 How large a number can you get?

Start with any six digits such as

$$5 \quad 3 \quad 9 \quad 7 \quad 2 \quad 4$$

and from them make two three-digit numbers, for example 324 and 579, where each digit has been used once only.

Now   (i) add your numbers   : $324 + 579 = 903$
         (ii) multiply your numbers: $324 \times 579 = 187\,596$

The object is to find as large a sum and as large a product as you can.

Can you decide on a strategy which would always give you the largest answers first time? If you can you can challenge your friend to see who can first find the largest number from a given set of six digits.

Variations on this would be to make up three two-digit numbers and look for the largest sum and product, or start with seven digits say and consider a three-digit and four-digit number.

118 Unit fractions

The Babylonians had no notation for a fraction such as $\frac{2}{3}$ or $\frac{3}{5}$ but only for unit fractions, that is fractions with 1 on the top, such as $\frac{1}{2}$ or $\frac{1}{5}$. This meant that a fraction like $\frac{2}{3}$ would have to be expressed as a sum or difference of unit fractions.

Thus

$$\frac{2}{3} = \frac{1}{3} + \frac{1}{3} \quad \text{or} \quad \frac{1}{3} + \frac{1}{6} + \frac{1}{6}$$

Can you find ways of expressing fractions as sums or differences of different unit fractions?

The following examples may give you some clues.

$$\frac{1}{3} - \frac{1}{4} = \frac{1}{12}$$

$$\frac{2}{5} = \frac{1}{5} + \frac{1}{6} + \frac{1}{30}$$

$$\frac{3}{4} = \frac{1}{4} + \frac{1}{5} + \frac{1}{6} + \frac{1}{20} + \frac{1}{24} + \frac{1}{30} + \frac{1}{120}$$

119 Four 4s

This well-tried activity has been responsible for many person-hours of interest and frustration. The idea is to express as many numbers as you can from 1 to 100 using exactly four 4s and any mathematical symbols you know.

For example

$$15 = \frac{44}{4} + 4 \quad \text{or} \quad (4 \times 4) - \frac{4}{4}$$

$$16 = (4 \times 4) + 4 - 4 \quad \text{or} \quad (4 \times \sqrt{4}) + (4 \times \sqrt{4})$$

There are often a number of ways of expressing the same number using four 4s as shown here but some numbers can be difficult to express. Apart from the four basic rules of +, −, ×, ÷ and $\sqrt{}$ illustrated here you may find the following helpful.

98

4! means 4 × 3 × 2 × 1 = 24 and is called 'factorial four'

$$\frac{4}{\cdot 4} = 10$$

$\cdot \dot{4}$ means 0.4 recurring and is equal to $\frac{4}{9}$

so $$\frac{4}{\cdot \dot{4}} = 9$$

You should now be able to find at least one way of expressing most, if not all, of the numbers from 1 to 100.

It may be fun to do this with a partner and challenge a pair of friends to see who can find the most in a given time.

120 Calculator words

Because of the way digits are formed on a calculator display they often look like letters when viewed upside down. Take, for example, the number 710.77345 which looks like this when displayed on a calculator.

Now view the display upside down and you should recognise a well-advertised petroleum product!

Because of this dual interpretation of the calculator display you can have a lot of interest and amusement.

Try 'translating' the following:

A calculator never tells 5317.

317537 went fishing off 3007 on a 0.717 for 3705 but only caught some 5733.

Instead of giving the numbers directly they can be replaced by calculations as the following passage illustrates.

(68 × 99) + 986 decided to (2486 + 3927 + 1322)

√(264 196) walking (10 609 × 5) because (21 386 ÷ 629)

had a (723 × 48) + 303   (85² + 109) in one and a

(2463 + 1977 − 736) in the other. They hurt like

(85² + 20² + 10² + 3²) and made him feel quite (2 × 5 × 7 × 11 + 1).

ShELL. OIL contains the additive Sh0ZZ.OIL. Remove it
and what do you get?

Make a list of the digits on your calculator which, with a
little imagination, can be interpreted as letters when viewed
upside down. You will be surprised how many there are.

Next make a word list using these letters and their number
equivalent. Do not forget that the order becomes reversed so
that, for example, the word 'heel' is not represented by 4337
but by 7334.

Now you are in a position to write your own story incor-
porating 'calculator words'. Replace the words by their
number equivalents or better, by calculations whose answer
gives the number equivalent.

121 Some calculator challenges

(i)   56 406 is the product of two consecutive numbers.
      What are the two numbers?
(ii) 357 627 is the product of three consecutive odd
      numbers. Find them!
(iii) 1405 is the sum of two consecutive square numbers.
      What are they?
(iv) The volume of a cube is 200 cubic centimetres. Find
      the length of the edge of the cube as accurately as you
      can with your calculator.

122 A calculator crossword

The clues are given below in two forms, in word form and number form.

When you have finished each calculation, turn your calculator display upside down to find the word.

Use the word clues and calculator clues to check each other.

Word clue	Calculation
Across	*Across*
2. Far from the truth.	2. $\sqrt{(100\,489)}$
4. A large edible bird.	4. $185^2 + 781$
6. 4 across might have produced many precious ones.	6. 809×7
7. At the heart of campanology.	7. $10127 - 2389$
8. Bisect Isis.	8. $(72 \times 323) \div 456$
9. Part of the ear.	9. $2^2 + 5^2 + 23^2 + 57^2$
12. Boy's name.	12. $(467 \times 680) - 23$
14. Help! not quite.	14. $3789 \div 7578$
Down	*Down*
1. Cavities.	1. $[(188 \times 463) \div 23 \cdot 5] + 50\,000$
2. A heron often stand on one.	2. $7^2 \times 13$
3. A close friend of 12 across.	3. $11\,545 + 7265 + 12763$
5. Traders do this.	5. $85^2 + 22^2 + 5^2 + 1^2$
7. The Good Book.	7. 198×191
10. Busy workers.	10. $(57 + 16)^2 + 3^2$
11. Exists.	11. $2856 \div 56$
13. . . . and behold!	13. $(28 \times 18) \div 720$

When you have completed this crossword, try constructing your own.

123 A mining bonanza

In the outback of Australia a mining company made test drillings into a rich mineral reserve. The evidence of the survey was mapped out on a square grid and the value, in millions of pounds, of the deposits indicated by numbers as shown above.

Because of the lie of the land and the open-cast mining method employed the company must begin at the square marked 'Start' and move from square to square either up or down, or across. Diagonal moves are not possible, and the same square cannot be mined twice.

Find the most profitable route for the miners for the first thirteen squares they mine.

One route for example could follow the squares
24 70 6 77 30 66 22 73 19 98 1 90 14
This would give a profit of £590 million.
You can do better!

32	80	19	98	1	90	14	85
66	22	73	52	72	57	83	31
30	84	41	73	16	74	45	92
77	6	70	24	Start	28	67	11
32	99	44	81	27	75	42	98
68	21	72	56	59	42	75	17
34	87	19	92	5	99	27	88

124 Hundreds, tens and units

Take any three-digit number such as 235. Write down the number formed by putting its digits in reverse order, 532.
Subtract the smaller number from the larger.

$$\begin{array}{r} 532 \\ - \ 235 \\ \hline 297 \end{array}$$

Now write down the number formed by reversing the order of the digits in the answer and add to the answer.

$$\begin{array}{r} 297 \\ + \ 792 \\ \hline 1089 \end{array}$$

When you have tried this on a few more numbers you should be able to predict the answer and baffle your friends.

125 Magic circles

Put the numbers 1, 2, 3, 4, 5, 6 into the squares so that the numbers on each circle add up to the same amount. When this happens the circles are said to be magic.

Can you find an easy rule for giving six other numbers which could be put in the squares to make the circles magic?

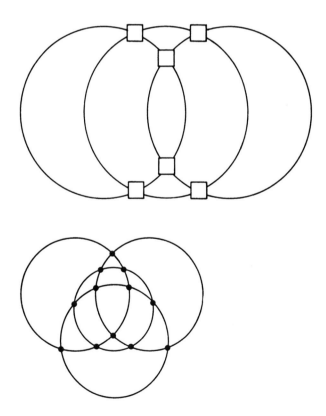

You should now be ready to tackle this magic circle puzzle for its solution is based on the same principle. Put one of the numbers 1, 2, 3, . . . , 10, 11, 12 at each intersection of the four circles in the diagram so that the circles are magic.

Is it obvious that the magic number for each circle is 39?

126 Number wheels

The three numbers of each spoke and each edge of the wheel all add up to the same number. What is the number?

Find all the missing numbers.

Now arrange the numbers 1 to 19 in a similar wheel so that the total along each of the twelve lines is 22.

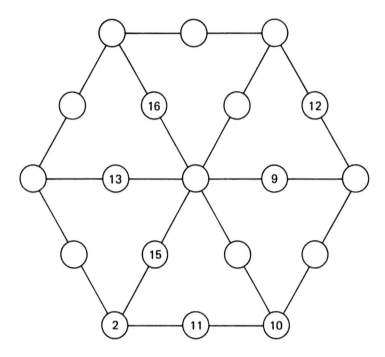

127 Make a century

By putting arithmetical signs in suitable places between the digits make the following sum correct:

   1   2   3   4   5   6   7   8   9   =   100

There is more than one solution. See how many you can find.

128 Division patterns

1 Use your calculator to work out

$$\frac{1}{7} \quad \frac{2}{7} \quad \frac{3}{7} \quad \frac{4}{7} \quad \frac{5}{7} \quad \frac{6}{7}$$

as decimal fractions.

What do you notice about the first six digits which occur after the decimal place?

Without using your calculator, write down the decimal fractions for $\frac{8}{7}, \frac{9}{7}, \frac{16}{7}$, to 6 decimal places.

If the calculator you were using had a longer display what would the first twelve digits be for $\frac{1}{7}$? Can you see how to write down the recurring pattern for any division by 7?

With any division sum it is a fact that the division process terminates at some stage or it generates a sequence of recurring digits, for example

$$\frac{3}{16} = 0.1875$$

$$\frac{3}{7} = 0.428\,571\,428\,571\,428\,571 \ldots$$

When dividing by a number which can be expressed as a power of 2 multiplied by a power of 5 such as 16, 20, 64, 125, 320 then the division process will always terminate. Why? However, when dividing by any other number the division process will always lead to a sequence of recurring digits. With division by 7 you will have found a pattern of six digits recurring, and in general on division by a number n the recurring pattern will be of length $n-1$ or less. Can you explain this?

2 A calculator was used to investigate the patterns of digits when dividing by 17 but its capacity was not large enough to exhibit the full cycle of repeating digits. The following calculations gave

$$\frac{1}{17} = 0.058\,823\,5$$

$$\frac{2}{17} = 0.117\,647\,1$$

$$\frac{3}{17} = 0.176\,470\,5$$

$$\frac{4}{17} = 0.235\,294\,1$$

$$\frac{5}{17} = 0.294\,117\,6$$

Knowing that in this case the repeating pattern has sixteen digits write down what the sequence of recurring digits will be and give $\frac{5}{17}$ as a decimal fraction to twenty decimal places. Try to predict $\frac{6}{17}, \frac{7}{17}$, etc. before checking with your calculator.

3 Try finding the repeating pattern of digits when dividing by 19 using as few calculator divisions as possible.

4 Now try finding patterns for division by other numbers, 11 and 13 for example are particularly interesting.

129 Prime numbers

Prime numbers are those whole numbers which are only divisible by 1 or themselves such as

5   29   41   83

The only even number which is prime is 2, for by definition all other even numbers such as 6, 10, 28, always have 2 as a factor in addition to 1 and themselves. It thus follows that apart from 2 all prime numbers must be odd.

Which numbers are prime and how they are distributed have fascinated mathematicians through the ages for they do not conform to any simple pattern. Theorems about them date back to Euclid in the third century BC when he produced an elegant proof that there are an infinity of primes.

Sometimes the primes follow one another very closely such as

2   3   5   7   11   13

but at other times they can be much more infrequent. There are only two primes between 23 and 37; what are they?

With numbers less than 100 you never have to go far from one prime to the next but the gaps between primes soon begin to widen after 100.

Find the next prime number after 113.

Even so with numbers less than 1000 it is rare to find ten consecutive numbers which do not contain a prime.

How many primes are there between 190 and 200?

In spite of this mathematicians have proved that there are sequences of consecutive whole numbers as long as you like to name (e.g. 5000) which do not contain a single prime number.

Many theorems about prime numbers have been suggested and generally accepted although many of them still await general proof.

1 One of these known as the Goldbach conjecture was suggested by Goldbach to Euler in 1742 with the request for a proof. He suggested that

> Every even number, other than 2, can be represented as the sum of two primes.

Euler could not prove this nor has anyone to this day, even though no exception to the theorem can be found.

Represent 28, 50, 100, 246 as the sum of two prime numbers. Is the representation unique?

2 Apart from 2, all the prime numbers are odd so that the difference between any two primes (other than 2) is an even number. That may be obvious but what is interesting is the belief that

> Every even number is the difference of two consecutive primes.

> Show that this is true for the even numbers

> 2   4   6   8   10   12   14

If you find the smallest primes in each case you will not need to exceed 250.

3 In 1848 de Polignac conjectured that

> Every odd number is the sum of a prime and a power of 2.

For example: $25 = 17 + 2^3$

Choose some odd numbers at random to test Polignac's conjecture. Is the representation unique?

4 Primes often seem to occur as pairs of consecutive odd numbers such as 5 and 7, 17 and 19, 29 and 31. It is believed that there is an infinity of such pairs but no-one has yet come near to proving it.

There are only three such pairs between 150 and 200. Find them!

5 Investigate the following conjectures.
  (i) There is at least one prime between consecutive square numbers.
  (ii) Every prime except 2 and 3 is of the form $6n \pm 1$ where n is a natural number.
  (iii) Any odd prime which is of the form $4n + 1$ is equal to the sum of two perfect squares.

130 Generating prime numbers

One of the problems in trying to prove results about the prime numbers is that the only way of deciding whether or not a number is prime is to find its factors. Through the ages people have searched in vain for formulae or routines which will generate primes and some of their better attempts are given here.

1 Consider the following sequence of primes and their differences

$$11 \quad 13 \quad 17 \quad 23 \quad 31 \quad \ldots$$
$$\quad 2 \quad\; 4 \quad\; 6 \quad\; 8$$

Continue this sequence as long as it generates primes.
   Because of the pattern of differences it shows that this sequence can be generated by the quadratic formula

$$n^2 + n + 11$$

2 Find the value of

$$n^2 + n + 41$$

for different values of n and check whether or not the number generated is prime or composite (has factors other than 1 and itself).
   This is a remarkable formula for it generates a prime number for all but seven of the numbers from 1 to 80. What is the first value of n for which $n^2 + n + 41$ is not prime?

3 An even better formula is

$$n^2 - 79n + 1601$$

for it gives a prime number for all whole number values of n up to 80.

4 What is the smallest value of n for which

$$2n^2 + 29$$

does not give a prime?

5 In 1640 the mathematician Fermat thought he had discovered a formula for generating prime numbers, namely

$$2^{2^n} + 1$$

   Find the numbers generated by this formula when $n = 0$, 1, 2, 3, 4. These numbers are prime.
   It took more than 100 years before the mathematician Euler showed that the number

$$2^{2^5} + 1$$

has the factors 641 and 6 700 417.

131 Some named numbers

Palindromic numbers

These are numbers such as 25452 which read the same forwards as backwards.

Not counting single-digit numbers, which is the smallest palindromic prime and which the smallest palindromic square number?

How many other palindromic square numbers are there less than 1000?

There are five palindromic primes between 100 and 200; which are they? Why are there no palindromic primes between 400 and 700? Show that all the palindromic numbers between 1000 and 2000 have a factor in common.

Excessive, perfect and defective numbers

Consider the number 8. Its factors, apart from 8 itself, are 1, 2, 4, and their sum is 7, which is less than 8. Because of this the Greek mathematicians classified 8 as an *excessive* number.

A number like 18, on the other hand, whose factors 1, 2, 3, 6, 9 total 21 they called a *defective* number.

Some numbers have the very special distinction of being equal to the sum of their factors. Such a number is 6 for its factors are 1, 2, 3. These numbers the Greeks called *perfect*.

(i) Classify the numbers less than 30 into these three categories.

(ii) Perfect numbers are few and far between. Euclid proved however that any number of the form

$$2^{n-1}(2^n - 1)$$

is perfect when $2^n - 1$ is prime.

Find values of n to make $2^n - 1$ prime and hence find some more perfect numbers.

Amicable pairs

Some pairs of numbers have the fascinating connection that the factor sum of each is equal to the other. This mutual support between two numbers has captured the imagination of some mathematicians who have named them *amicable pairs*.

The smallest such pair is 220 and 284.

$$220 : 1 + 2 + 4 + 5 + 10 + 11 + 20 + 22 + 44 + 55 + 110 = 284$$

$$284 : 1 + 2 + 4 + 71 + 142 = 220$$

Euler made a study of such pairs and in 1750 published a list of 60 of them. Surprisingly he missed the second smallest pair, 1184 and 1210, and these were not discovered until 1866 when a 16 year old boy Paganini found them.

Find the divisors of this pair and check their close interconnection.

Further pairs to investigate are

2620	6232	17 296
2924	6368	18 416

132 Further number patterns

1 $3^2 - 2^2 = 9 - 4 = 5 = 3 + 2$
   $4^2 - 3^2 = 16 - 9 = 7 = 4 + 3$
   $5^2 - 4^2 = 25 - 16 = 9 = 5 + 4$

   Explain the pattern and show that it is always true.

2 $3^2 = 9$ $2 \times 4 = 8$
   $4^2 = 16$ $3 \times 5 = 15$
   $5^2 = 25$ $4 \times 6 = 24$

   Extend the pattern. Is it true for large numbers?

3 Investigate the successive powers of a whole number
   such as 3 3^2 3^3 3^4 3^5 ...

   In particular note the pattern formed by the last digit.

4 Complete the following and continue for two more lines:

$$1 =$$
$$3 + 5 =$$
$$7 + 9 + 11 =$$
$$13 + 15 + 17 + 19 =$$

   Can you make a general statement to describe the pattern?

5 Complete the following patterns and make an observation
   on what you find:

$$1 = \qquad\qquad 1^3 =$$
$$1 + 2 = \qquad\qquad 1^3 + 2^3 =$$
$$1 + 2 + 3 = \qquad\qquad 1^3 + 2^3 + 3^3 =$$
$$1 + 2 + 3 + 4 = \qquad\qquad 1^3 + 2^3 + 3^3 + 4^3 =$$

133 Pythagorean triads

Pythagoras' theorem relating the lengths of the sides of a right-angled triangle is well known (see also Activity 64). Also widely known is the fact that a triangle whose sides are in the ratio $3 : 4 : 5$ is right-angled as $3^2 + 4^2 = 5^2$.

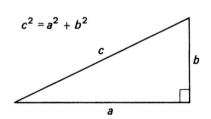

$c^2 = a^2 + b^2$

The Pythagorean triads are sets of whole numbers like 3, 4 and 5 which satisfy the relation $a^2 + b^2 = c^2$ and can thus be used as the lengths of sides for a right-angled triangle.

Use your calculator to produce a table of the squares of the numbers from 1 to 50 and see how many triads you can find.

Can you find two different right-angled triangles with whole-number sides whose areas are equal?

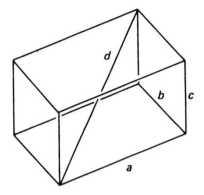

A similar problem in three dimensions is to find possible lengths for the edges of a cuboid (i.e. a rectangular box) so that the edges and the diagonal are all whole numbers.

$$a^2 + b^2 + c^2 = d^2$$

One solution is

$$1^2 + 2^2 + 2^2 = 3^2$$

Can you find some more?

134 Guess the rule

One person A acts as a computer which is programmed to compute a new number from any number given to him. The others in turn give A a number x which he processes, using the rule on which he has decided, and records both it and the number y he has computed from it for all to see. The object is to guess the rule being used by A but before being allowed a guess a person must give a number x and declare correctly the number y which A would compute from it.

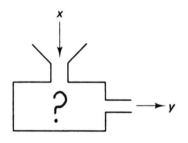

Here are some suggestions for rules to get you started.
Double the number.
Add 3 to the number.
Square the number.
Multiply by the next number.
Multiply by the previous number.
Take the next odd number.
Take the next prime number.
Double and add 1.
Take the next number if the given number is even but the previous number if the given number is odd.
Give the sum of its prime factors.
Square and take away 1.
Give the sum of the digits forming the number.
Take the number from 100.

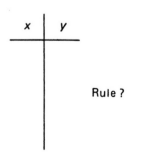

Another version of the game is to have two input numbers x and y, and A then has some rule to combine them.

Yet another version is for A to have a set of numbers in mind, say the multiples of 3, and the other players suggest numbers which A replies by saying *in* or *out* depending on whether they are in his set or not. The object is now to decide on what set of numbers A has in mind. In playing this version it is helpful to decide beforehand to limit the numbers to say 0 to 100 and for the sets thought of by A to have several members so that a reasonable proportion of the numbers suggested by the players will be in A's set.

135 Intriguing multiplications

Playing with his calculator one day Johnny multiplied together the numbers 159 and 48 and obtained 7632. On reflection he realised that the equation

$$159 \times 48 = 7632$$

contained each of the digits 1, 2, ..., 9 once only. He could hardly believe his luck and felt the result must be unique. But he was wrong! There are several other pairs of numbers whose product gives a sum which uses all the digits only once. Can you find any of them?

Another intriguing product is

$$16\,583\,742 \times 9 = 149\,253\,678$$

where all the digits occur once on each side of the equality sign. Can you find any other products with this property?

136 Equate the diagonals

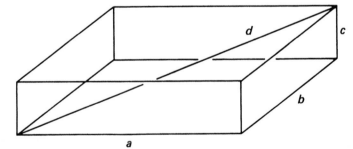

The edges of a box are of length a, b and c units where a, b, c are whole numbers. Using Pythagoras' theorem it is easy to show that if d is the length of the diagonal then

$$d^2 = a^2 + b^2 + c^2$$

Show that a box with dimensions 4, 5 and 6 units has the same length diagonal as a box with dimensions 2, 3 and 8 units.

Find other pairs of boxes whose edges are a whole number of units and whose diagonals are equal. There are at least three more solutions where all the edges are less than 10 units.

137 Magic stars

Put numbers in the empty circles of stars (a) and (b) so that
the numbers along each line of *both* stars have the same total.

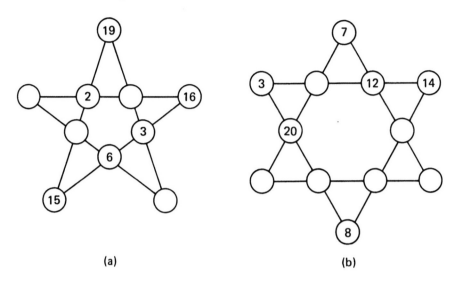

(a) (b)

Stars (c) and (d) are also magic (i.e. the numbers along each
line have the same total) and each have the same magic
number. Further, the missing numbers in each case are 1, 3,
4, 5, and 7. What more help do you want!

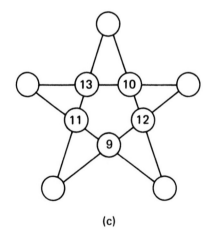

(c)

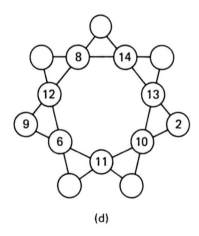

(d)

138 Safety first

(a) is an addition sum in disguise. Each letter stands for a
different digit. S, for example, represents 3. What do the
other letters represent?
   (b) is another classic problem of the same kind.

```
    C R O S S
  +   R O A D S
  -------------
    D A N G E R
```
(a)

```
    S E N D
  + M O R E
  ---------
  M O N E Y
```
(b)

139 The gambler's secret strategy

A gambler made three dice.
The red dice had the numbers 2, 4, 9 twice on its faces.
The blue dice had the numbers 3, 5, 7 twice on its faces.
The yellow dice had the numbers 1, 6, 8 twice on its faces.

The total on the faces of each dice was the same but the gambler was confident that if he let his opponent choose a dice first and roll it he could select a dice which would give him a better chance of obtaining a higher score. Explain!

140 The transportation problem

Three bus companies Aristotle, Bacchus and Copernicus provide the buses to transport the children home from the four schools, Piltdown, Queen's, Ruritania and Scholars.

To transport all the children the number of buses required at the schools are

   P: 8   Q: 5   R: 7   S: 5

and the bus companies have suitable buses at their depots as follows:

   A: 9   B: 6   C: 10

	P	Q	R	S	Available buses
A	3	1	5		9
B			2	4	6
C	5	4		1	10
Buses required	8	5	7	5	

The first table shows one of the many possible ways in which the bus companies could allocate their buses to the schools.

The next table shows the distance in miles from the bus depots to the schools, for example it shows that from C to Q is 6 miles.

Naturally the education authority wishes to keep its costs as low as possible so it wants to find the best way of allocating the buses from the depots to the schools so as to reduce the total mileage covered.

	P	Q	R	S
A	3	2	5	1
B	2	1	3	4
C	5	6	4	8

The above allocation gives a total bus mileage of

$$(3 \times 3) + (1 \times 2) + (5 \times 5) + (2 \times 3) + (4 \times 4) + (5 \times 5) + (4 \times 6) + (1 \times 8)$$

$$= \quad 9 \quad + \quad 2 \quad + \quad 25 \quad + \quad 6 \quad + \quad 16 \quad + \quad 25 \quad + \quad 24 \quad + \quad 8$$

$$= 115 \text{ miles}$$

By making better use of the shorter routes the total mileage can be much reduced. In fact it can be made as low as 67 miles. How?

141 'Mind reading' number cards

Imagine you had a set of weights consisting of one each of

$$1 \text{ kg} \quad 2 \text{ kg} \quad 4 \text{ kg} \quad 8 \text{ kg} \quad 16 \text{ kg}$$

With these it would be possible to weigh any whole number of kilograms from 1 kg to 31 kg.

Copy and complete the following table up to 31 to show which weights are used.

	16	8	4	2	1
1					✓
2				✓	
3				✓	✓
4			✓		
5			✓		✓
6			✓	✓	
7			✓	✓	✓
8		✓			
9		✓			✓
10		✓		✓	
11		✓		✓	✓
12		✓	✓		
13		✓	✓		✓
14		✓	✓	✓	
15		✓	✓	✓	✓
16	✓				
17	✓				✓

Now cut out five squares of card say 10 cm × 10 cm and with a felt pen on the first card put clearly all the numbers which correspond to a mass which needed the 1 kg weight. The result is shown here in the diagram.

1	3	5	7
9	11	13	15
17	19	21	23
25	27	29	31

On the second card put all the numbers which correspond to a mass which needed the 2 kg weight (i.e. 2, 3, 6, 7, 10, 11, etc.); on the third card put all the numbers which correspond to a mass which needed the 4 kg weight in its weighing, and so on.

You should now have five cards each with sixteen numbers on them. To check that you have them right, turn to the back of this book.

The game is to ask a friend to think of a number from 1 to 31 and then show him each of your cards in turn. If his number is on a card he is to respond 'Yes', if not, 'No'. By the time he has finished saying 'Yes' or 'No' to the last card you should be able to tell him the number he had thought of! 'How?' you may well ask.

Suppose your friend thinks of 21, then this will be on three cards, the 1 kg card, the 4 kg card and the 16 kg card. All you do is add together 1 + 4 + 16, the cards to which your friend responded 'Yes' to, and you will have 21. To help it is useful to put a 1, 2, 4, 8 or 16 on the back of the appropriate card so that you can see it, but small enough so that your friend will probably not notice it. You can then shuffle the cards in any order and not look at the side you show your friend at all which will baffle him even more.

Try to practise the use of your cards with someone else in the family so you develop a slick technique before trying it on your friends.

You can start again and make a table up to 63 using one additional weight of 32 kg. Then you will need six cards with 32 numbers on each.

142 3 × 3 magic squares

A magic square is a square of numbers in which every row, column and diagonal add up to the same total such as the example in (a) where every line totals 24, its magic number.

Complete magic squares (b) and (c) by first finding their magic numbers from the completed line of numbers.

11	3	10
7	8	9
6	13	5

(a)

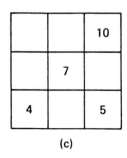

6		
7	5	3

(b)

		10
	7	
4		5

(c)

Now try (d) and (e), where more numbers are given to you but the reasoning is not so straightforward.

14	3	
		13
8	15	

(d)

11	1	
9		7
	15	5

(e)

The formation of magic squares is an ancient pastime and records of them go back in China to before Christ. The basic 3×3 square for example is attributed to the Chinese Emperor Yu who reigned around 2200 BC. Their fascination has not diminished with time as recent books on the subject testify.

All 3×3 magic squares have essentially one pattern which is that of the square formed from the numbers 1, 2, 3, . . . , 9 (see (f)).

8	1	6
3	5	7
4	9	2

(f)

Other magic squares could be formed from this by, for example, increasing all the numbers by a given number, say 6. Alternatively the numbers 1 to 9 could be replaced by the first nine odd numbers 1, 3, 5, . . . , 17.

There is another interesting way for generating a set of nine numbers which will form a 3×3 magic square which is not so obvious.

Take any number to start (e.g. 3), then decide on two different numbers (e.g. 2 and 5) which will be added to the original number as shown below.

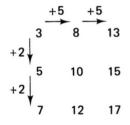

Now take these numbers in the order

3 8 13 5 10 15 7 12 17

and in this order replace the numbers 1 to 9 in the basic square. The result is magic square (g) with magic number 30.

Now produce some magic squares of your own.

Would this method work with decimal numbers or some negative numbers?

Can you prove it to be generally true?

12	3	15
13	10	7
5	17	8

(g)

143 4 × 4 and higher order magic squares

The first evidence of magic squares being investigated in Europe was in the early part of the fifteenth century. Agrippa constructed magic squares of all orders from 3 to 9 which he associated with the earth's planets then known. People through the ages have always held a mysticism for numbers (we still say 'third time lucky' and often believe 13 to be unlucky, for example) and magic squares have their own particular aura. The artist Dürer did a woodcut which he called *Melancholy* in which the date of its execution 1514 appears as part of a 4×4 magic square in the picture.

16	3	2	13
5	10	11	8
9	6	7	12
4	15	14	1

In this magic square the rows, columns and main diagonals all total 34. There are also many other sets of four symmetrically placed numbers in the square which total 34 such as

16   13   4   1   and   3   8   14   9

What other sets can you find?

With the numbers 1, 2 . . . , 16 it is possible to make 880 fundamentally different 4×4 magic squares. These were first all published in 1693 by Frénicle. Not all these possess all the symmetries of Dürer's square above. Some, classified as *simple*, possess only the basic requirement to be magic while others, classified as Nasik, are considered the most perfect and contain even more symmetry than Dürer's square. Here are examples of each.

7	6	11	10
14	9	8	3
12	15	2	5
1	4	13	16

Simple

1	14	7	12
15	4	9	6
10	5	16	3
8	11	2	13

Nasik

Find as many sets of four symmetrically placed numbers in each which total 34. Make yourself some square counters, number them 1 to 16 and see how many different 4×4 magic squares you can find.

There are no particularly neat ways of constructing magic squares of even order but with squares of odd order the following method due to Bachet de Méziriac is worth knowing. It is illustrated here for a 5×5 magic square but is equally applicable to any odd order.

3	16	9	22	15
20	8	21	14	2
7	25	13	1	19
24	12	5	18	6
11	4	17	10	23

←

The diamond arrangement (numbered along diagonals):

```
                    5
                4       10
        3       9       15
    2       8       14       20
1       7       13       19       25
    6       12       18       24
        11      17      23
            16      22
                21
```

First border the 5×5 square as shown to produce a diamond shape. Now number the diagonals from far left to top right as shown. Next imagine sliding the numbers outside the original square into the spaces on the opposite side of the square without changing their arrangement. The result is a magic square.

One magic square which deserves a special mention is Euler's 8 × 8 solution which is also a knight's tour (see Activity 89). It was obviously not known to H. E. Dudeney the famous Victorian puzzler who, writing about the possibility of such a magic square existing, says 'Can a perfect solution be found? I am convinced that it cannot, but it is only a pious opinion.'

119

144 Multigrades

In magic square (a) it is true of necessity that

$$8 + 1 + 6 = 4 + 9 + 2$$

but what you probably had not realised is the additional property that

$$8^2 + 1^2 + 6^2 = 4^2 + 9^2 + 2^2$$

Similarly

$$8 + 3 + 4 = 6 + 7 + 2$$

and

$$8^2 + 3^2 + 4^2 = 6^2 + 7^2 + 2^2$$

Does this work for other 3x3 magic squares? Check that in (b) and (c) once again the sums of the squares of the numbers in the outside rows (or columns) are equal. Is it always true?

Sets of numbers such as these where not only their sums but the sums of some other powers are equal are called *multigrades*. The ones so far considered are called second-order multigrades but the following is an example of a third-order multigrade as it is true for three powers:

$$1 + 5 + 8 + 12 = 2 + 3 + 10 + 11$$
$$1^2 + 5^2 + 8^2 + 12^2 = 2^2 + 3^2 + 10^2 + 11^2$$
$$1^3 + 5^3 + 8^3 + 12^3 = 2^3 + 3^3 + 10^3 + 11^3$$

With such a fascinating relation between the sets of numbers you may think they would be difficult to find but this is not so.

Suppose we increase each of the numbers in the last example by 2 then clearly

$$3 + 7 + 10 + 14 = 4 + 5 + 12 + 13$$

but surprisingly

$$3^2 + 7^2 + 10^2 + 14^2 = 4^2 + 5^2 + 12^2 + 13^2$$

and

$$3^3 + 7^3 + 10^3 + 14^3 = 4^3 + 5^3 + 12^3 + 13^3$$

Investigate the effect of adding some other numbers. But how do we construct a multigrade from scratch? Start with a simple equality such as

$$1 + 5 = 2 + 4$$

Add 5 to each term: $6 + 10 = 7 + 9$

8	1	6
3	5	7
4	9	2

(a)

9	2	10
8	7	6
4	12	5

(b)

12	5	15
13	10	7
5	17	8

(c)

Swop sides and combine to give a second order multigrade:

$$1 \; + 5 \; + 7 \; + 9 \; = 2 \; + 4 \; + 6 \; + 10$$

and

$$1^2 + 5^2 + 7^2 + 9^2 \; = \; 2^2 + 4^2 + 6^2 + 10^2$$

The number 5 which was added to each term was the smallest which would ensure that all the numbers in the multigrade were different.

To form a third-order multigrade use the same process as before but on the second-order multigrade.

Add 10 to each of the numbers above to obtain

$$11 + 15 + 17 + 19 \; = \; 12 + 14 + 16 + 20$$

then swop and add to get

$$1^n + 5^n + 7^n + \; 9^n + 12^n + 14^n + 16^n + 20^n$$

$$= \; 2^n + 4^n + 6^n + 10^n + 11^n + 15^n + 17^n + 19^n$$

when $n = 1$, 2 or 3. Use your calculator to check that this is correct.

Suppose that from the starting point of

$$1 + 5 \; = \; 2 + 4$$

4 had been added instead of 5 as above, then this would result in the second-order multigrade based on the sets

$$(1, 5, 6, 8) \quad \text{and} \quad (2, 4, 5, 9)$$

which reduces to

$$(1, 6, 8) \quad \text{and} \quad (2, 4, 9)$$

as 5 is in common.

This is in fact the multigrade associated with the 3×3 magic square at the beginning.

Now add 5 to the numbers in these sets and with the usual process this gives the third-order multigrade

$$(1, 6, 8, 7, 9, 14) \quad \text{and} \quad (2, 4, 9, 6, 11, 13)$$

but as 6 and 9 are common it follows that

$$1 \; + 8 \; + 7 \; + 14 \; = \; 2 \; + 4 \; + 11 \; + 13$$

$$1^2 + 8^2 + 7^2 + 14^2 \; = \; 2^2 + 4^2 + 11^2 + 13^2$$

$$1^3 + 8^3 + 7^3 + 14^3 \; = \; 2^3 + 4^3 + 11^3 + 13^3$$

Try inventing your own multigrades. By repeating the process shown here you can easily generate fourth- and fifth-order multigrades or even higher orders.

145 Pascal's triangle

This triangular array of numbers known as Pascal's triangle, after the French mathematician and philosopher Blaise Pascal, is probably familiar to you but how much do you know about it?

Can you give the next two lines?

Find the sum of the numbers in each row and make a guess as to the sum of the numbers in the twelfth row. This pattern occurs in many situations several of which will now be described so that you can investigate them for yourself.

```
              1
            1   1
          1   2   1
        1   3   3   1
      1   4   6   4   1
    1   5  10  10   5   1
```

Tossing a coin

Suppose a penny is tossed four times. The sixteen different ways in which the sequence of heads (H) and tails (T) could occur are recorded below showing first the sequence with all heads, then the sequence with three heads and so on up to no heads.

Four heads	Three heads	Two heads	One head	No head
HHHH	HHHT	HHTT	HTTT	TTTT
	HHTH	HTHT	THTT	
	HTHH	TTHH	TTTH	
	THHH	HTTH	TTHT	
		THHT		
		THTH		
1	4	6	4	1

The numbers of arrangements correspond to the fifth row of Pascal's triangle. Try investigating arrangements with a coin tossed twice, three times, and five times.

Powers of 11

$$
\begin{aligned}
11^0 &= \quad\quad\quad 1 \\
11^1 &= \quad\quad 1 \quad 1 \\
11^2 &= \quad 1 \quad 2 \quad 1 \\
11^3 &= 1 \quad 3 \quad 3 \quad 1
\end{aligned}
$$

At which stage does the pattern cease to look like Pascal's triangle and why?

Hexagonal maze

Sixteen rats enter a hexagonal maze as shown and at each fork half go one way and half go the other.

How many leave the maze at p, q, r, s and t? Try with 32 entering a maze which extends one more stage.

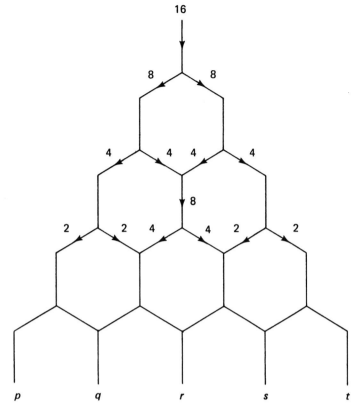

A practical demonstration of this can be seen with a *Quincunx*. This is a sloping board with nails sticking out of it at points corresponding to the vertices of the hexagonal network. Balls are rolled down the slope toward the single nail at the top and on average half the balls rolled are deflected by it to the right, half to the left. The size of the balls in relation to the distances between the nails is such that the rolling balls hit succeeding pins symmetrically.

Shortest routes on the streets of New York

The streets of New York form a rectangular grid as shown.

From the start to A the shortest route is straight along and there are no other routes of the same length.

From the start to B however there are six different routes involving 2 units across and 2 down. The number of shortest routes to some of the street intersections is show shown. Find the missing ones. Can you spot the Pascal's triangle pattern?

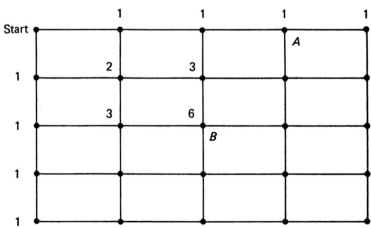

Cuisenaire rods

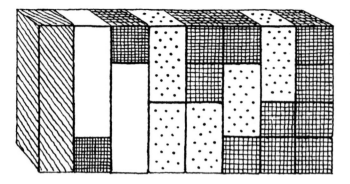

Some of you may be familiar with Cuisenaire rods. These are colour-coded blocks of wood of lengths 1, 2, 3, 4, 5 etc. used to help teach children basic number concepts. The diagram here shows all the eight possible ways of arranging the rods to make a length corresponding to the number 4.

> There is 1 way with 1 rod.
> There are 3 ways with 2 rods.
> There are 3 ways with 3 rods.
> There is 1 way with 4 rods.

Consider the different ways to use the rods to represent 5.

The binomial pattern

$$(1 + a)^0 = 1$$
$$(1 + a)^1 = 1 + a$$
$$(1 + a)^2 = 1 + 2a + a^2$$
$$(1 + a)^3 = 1 + 3a + 3a^2 + a^3$$
$$(1 + a)^4 = 1 + 4a + 6a^2 + 4a^3 + a^4$$

When expanding algebraic expressions like $(1 + a)^n$, where n is a positive whole number, the coefficients always correspond to the number in a row of Pascal's triangle.

Sets of numbers in Pascal's triangle

A variety of sets of numbers can be detected in Pascal's triangle by looking along the diagonals.

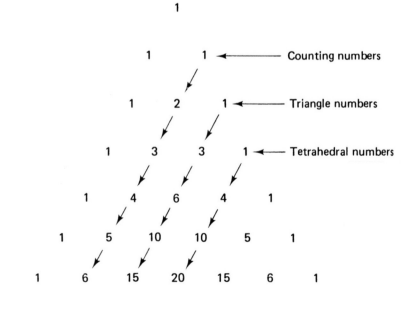

Also the sum of the numbers along a diagonal is always equal to the next number in the adjacent diagonal at every stage. For example

$$1 + 2 + 3 + 4 + 5 = 15$$
$$1 + 3 + 6 + 10 \quad\quad = 20$$
$$1 + 4 + 10 \quad\quad\quad = 15$$

Modifications of Pascal's triangle can be investigated to see if anything of interest materialises such as the following.

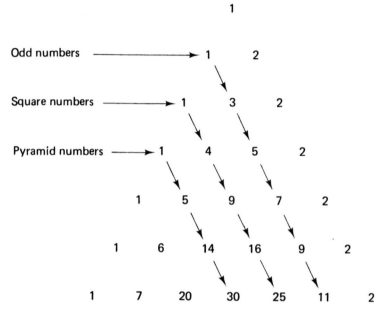

146 Generating Fibonacci sequences

Sticking stamps

Suppose you had a large supply of 1p and 2p postage stamps. How many different ways could you stick the stamps across the top of a postcard (side by side and the right way up) to total 1p, 2p, 3p, 4p, 5p, etc.?

For example to total 4p five arrangements are possible.

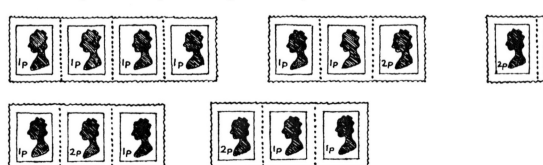

Climbing stairs

Somewhat similar is the question of how many ways a person can run up a given number of stairs if he can take one or two steps at a time.

Spiralling squares

A rather different example is to make a note of the largest side of the rectangle formed at each stage in the construction opposite.

Start with a square with 1 cm side and add an equal square to form a 2 × 1 rectangle. Add a 2 × 2 square to its largest side to form a 3 × 2 rectangle, then a 3 × 3 square to the new rectangle's largest side to form a 5 × 3 rectangle and so on.

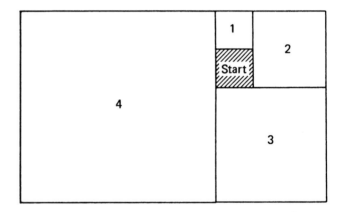

Pascal's triangle

Total the numbers along the lines shown in Pascal's triangle.

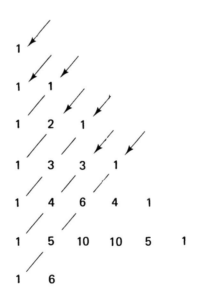

The Fibonacci sequence

In the examples above you should have found the numbers of the following sequence:

1 1 2 3 5 8 13 ...

where the next number is formed by adding together the previous two. For example 13 = 5 + 8 and the next number will be 8 + 13 = 21. This sequence is the one commonly known as the Fibonacci sequence.

What is the sequence formed from the differences between successive numbers in this case?

There is a nice relation connecting each group of three successive numbers other than the fact that the third is the sum of the previous two. Can you find it?

The number sequence occurs in nature in many surprising ways. If you look at the scales on a fir cone you will see that they appear to spiral around the cone. Now count the number of such spirals and you will always find it is equal to one of the numbers in the Fibonacci sequence. Similarly the seeds in a sunflower head also lie on spirals and the number of spirals will again be a Fibonacci number.

The rectangle construction in 'spiralling squares' gives a very practical way of drawing a spiral by drawing a quadrant of a circle in each new square which is added.

On squared paper make a copy of the rectangle construction, continue it as far as your paper will allow and then draw in the spiral.

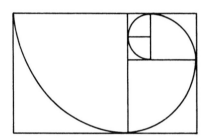

147 Fibonacci sequences and the golden section ratio

Sequence: 1   1   2   3   5   8   13   21
Ratios: $\frac{1}{1}$ $\frac{2}{1}$ $\frac{3}{2}$ $\frac{5}{3}$ $\frac{8}{5}$ $\frac{13}{8}$ $\frac{21}{13}$

Use your calculator to express the ratios in decimal form. What do you notice?

Now take any two numbers as a starting point and generate a Fibonacci sequence from them by using the rule of always adding the last two numbers. Again form the ratios.

For example starting with 2 and 9:

Fibonacci sequence: 2   9   11   20   31   51   82   133

$\frac{9}{2}$ $\frac{11}{9}$ $\frac{20}{11}$ $\frac{31}{20}$ $\frac{51}{31}$ $\frac{82}{51}$ $\frac{133}{82}$

No matter what numbers you start with you should have found that your ratios appear to be always getting closer and closer to a number which starts 1.618 03 . . .

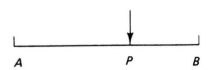

This number was studied by the Greeks in a geometrical context. They wanted to divide a line segment AB at a point P so that the ratio $AP : PB$ equalled $AB : AP$.

This ratio is called the *golden section* ratio and its precise value is given by $\frac{1}{2}(1 + \sqrt{5})$. Can you show this?

Interestingly too it is the ratio of a diagonal to the side of a regular pentagon and this fact makes it possible to construct a regular pentagon using only a pencil, ruler and compass. Can you do it?

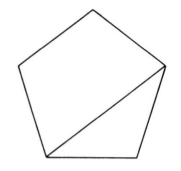

Psychologists have done experiments which suggest that people find the most pleasing rectangular shape is that with its sides in the golden section ratio. Artists too have been fascinated by this ratio as have architects and used it in the design of their pictures or buildings. Interestingly if you start with a rectangle whose lengths are in the golden section ratio then cutting a square off it leaves a smaller rectangle whose sides are also in the golden section ratio.

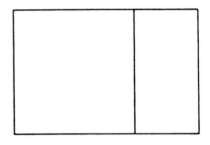

By inventing rules similar to the Fibonacci rule other interesting sequences can be generated. For example start with two numbers and always form the next number from the sum of the previous number and twice the one before that:

1   1   3   5   11   21   43   85   . . .

What happens to successive ratios now?

148 A weighing problem

A greengrocer had a pair of scales and four weights. The weights were such that with them he could correctly weigh any whole number of kilograms from 1 to 40.

How heavy was each weight and how could he manage to weigh all the different weights?

149 Similar rectangles

A sheet of rectangular paper is such that when it is folded in half it forms a rectangle of exactly the same shape as the original. What can be said about the lengths of its sides?

150 A magic cube

27 unit cubes are numbered from 1 to 27. There are several ways in which they can be made into a 3 × 3 × 3 cube so that any row of unit cubes parallel to an edge of the main cube correspond to numbers which total 42. The long diagonals of the cube also total 42 but not the diagonals of the faces. The diagram shows the arrangement for the top layer for one solution. Can you find the arrangements for the other two layers?

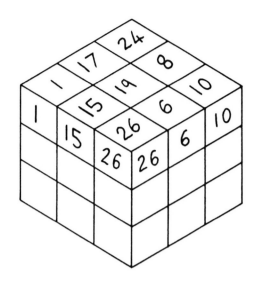

151 A question of balance

In a box there are 27 new red snooker balls all looking exactly alike. However it is known that one of them is faulty and weighs more than the others. Given that you have a balance but no weights show how, by comparing sets of balls against each other, you can find the faulty ball in only three balances.

152 Further calculator challenges

(i)   What is the remainder on dividing 89 328 by 729?
(ii) Find a way of using the $\sqrt{}$ function to help in evaluating $\sqrt[3]{200}$.
(iii) What is the smallest number x which gives the answer 0 to the calculation $1/x$ on your calculator?

153 The only magic hexagon

Fill in the hexagons with the numbers 1, 2, 3, . . . , 19 so that the total of the numbers on every vertical path and on every diagonal path is always the same.

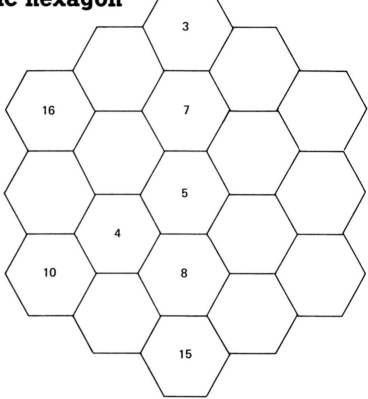

154 Nim

The game of Nim is for two people and appears to be simplicity itself. You need a supply of counters (matchsticks or drawing pins would do) and the game starts with the counters arranged arbitrarily in a number of heaps. In the example shown here there are three heaps with 7, 9 and 6 counters.

Each player in turn can remove as many counters as he likes from one of the heaps (he can if he wishes remove all the counters in a heap, but he must take at least one). The winner is the player who removes the last counter.

There is much more to this game than might first appear. See if you can develop some winning strategy.

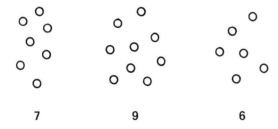

7   9   6

130

COMMENTARY

Activity 1

The same solution works for each case.

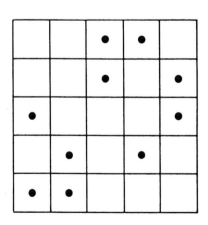

No counters can be added to (d) or (e) but three can be added to (f) as shown here.

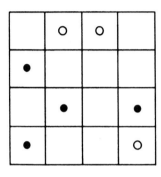

(f)

The solutions to the 4 x 4 board illustrate a degree of symmetry often found in the 'best' solution. Note also that it occurs in (d) and (e) which might be described as the 'worst' solutions. This phenomenon is common to many mathematical problems of this kind.

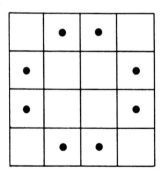 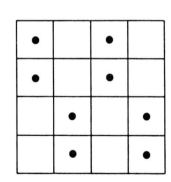

Solutions to 4 x 4 board

Solution to 5 x 5 board

133

Activity 2

The solution shown here for the classical chessboard problem again shows a line of symmetry.

This problem and the previous activity are all based on the fact that it is possible to place $2n$ counters on an $n \times n$ board so that no three counters are in line.

Activity 3

This game is closely related to the previous two activities but is complementary to it. Here, a player's strategy is to look for positions of the pieces which limit his opponent's play and force him into making a move with three in a line.

Activities 4, 5 and 6

Approximating to a curved path as a sequence of small steps is of fundamental importance in mathematics and is at the heart of calculus and numerical methods. The result not only makes an attractive drawing but can also be produced using coloured thread or wool (i) stitched through a piece of card or (ii) stretched between panel pins (i.e. small nails) hammered into a piece of plywood. In these activities a new line cannot be drawn until the previous one has been completed. They should not be confused with the more familiar ones where an equal number of points is marked off on two lines (or curves) to start with and then the points joined by lines as shown in the two examples here.

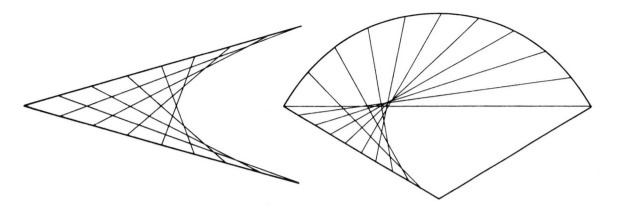

Activity 7

This is an easy puzzle of its **kind. The** two pieces are each
equivalent to a square and **half a square** as shown. It is
surprising how many shapes **can be** made from them. To
achieve all the shapes shown **one of** the pieces will need to be
turned over. Which of the shapes can be made without doing
this?

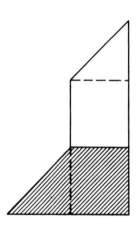

Activity 8

If you could do this correctly without a model you have a
good spatial sense.

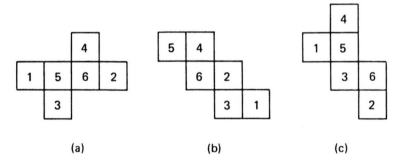

(a) (b) (c)

Activity 9

The secret here is to think three-dimensionally and form a
tetrahedron.

Activity 10

Triangular sheep pens may be unorthodox but it solves the problem.

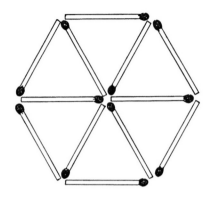

Activity 11

Number the map on both sides then fold as shown below.

Then partly open out and pinching together 5 and 4 fold them so that 5 comes next to 6. 4 will then be next to 3 and it is an easy matter to pinch 1 and 2 together and fold them so that 1 is on top of 2 and 2 on top of 3.

Activity 12

The showman must first take the goat across. He then takes the wolf across and brings the goat back. He next takes the cabbage across and finally returns to collect the goat.

Activities 13, 14, 15, 16 and 17

These show a variety of ways of producing an ellipse. Activity 13 shows how an ellipse is, in effect, a circle stretched in one direction. Activity 14 shows the ellipse as a circle viewed from an angle – we rarely see a circle but we have learned to interpret the ellipses we see as representing circular objects. Activity 15 is a nice way of producing an ellipse by folding paper along lines which touch it. This activity along with Activity 16 automatically locates the two focal points of the ellipse. Activity 17 gives an example of the ellipse as the path of a point on a moving object and there are many situations where this happens. There are many other interesting constructions for drawing ellipses and the reader is recommended to look for books on engineering drawing. Historically the ellipse is very interesting for John Kepler (1571–1630) deduced correctly, from his astronomical observations, that *every* planet moves in an ellipse with the sun at one focus. Today we are familiar with the idea of artificial satellites 'circling' the earth but how many people realise that they travel an elliptic orbit with the earth at a focus.

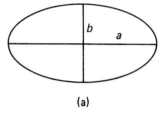

(a)

In activity 13, if the longest radius of an ellipse is a and the shortest radius is b it can be shown that its area is πab. Thus in an ellipse where $a = 2b$, its area is $2\pi b^2$ which is twice the area of the circle from which it was obtained. Similarly, if a circle is stretched three times in one direction its area is trebled.

The perimeter of the ellipse cannot be found nearly as easily and there is no exact formula for it. When the ellipse is not too elongated $\pi(a + b)$ gives a reasonable approximation to its perimeter. But, in general, a much better approximation is that given by Ramanujan in 1914, namely
$$\pi \{3(a + b) - \sqrt{[(a + 3b)(3a + b)]}\} \ .$$

Activity 18

This game must end in a limited number of moves because it starts with nine available arms (three points each with three arms) and each move uses up two arms and introduces a new point with one available arm. The effect of a move is thus to reduce the total number of available arms by one. There can thus be at most eight moves. There may be a fewer number of moves if one arm becomes isolated by the rest of the network.

These networks correspond to the different ways in which chemical atoms with a valency of 3 can join to make complex molecules.

Activity 19

A and D are the same.

Activity 20

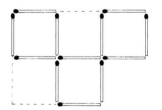 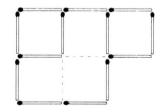

Activity 21

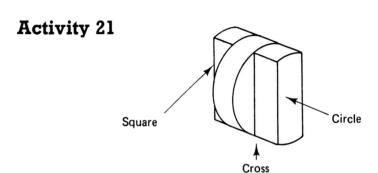

Square

Circle

Cross

Activity 22

This puzzle can seem quite impossible until you find the
solution. It has much in common with Activity 33. The key
is to shunt C onto the main line by itself as shown below.

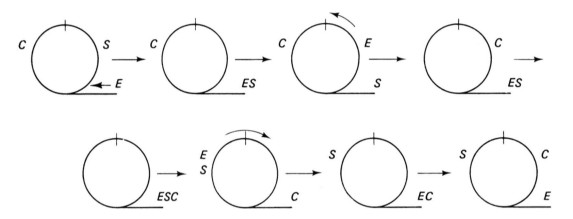

Activity 23

First fill the 3 pt jug. Next pour the 3 pints from this jug
into the 5 pt jug. Again fill the 3 pt jug and then pour from
it into the partially filled 5 pt jug until it is full. This leaves
exactly 1 pint in the 3 pt jug.

It would thus be possible to measure any whole number of
pints by measuring single pints in this way. Clearly there are
more efficient ways for measuring most quantities. 5 pints and
3 pints can be measured directly and as 6 = 3 + 3 while 8 =
5 + 3, 6 pints and 8 pints are easily measured. But what about
7 pints and 4 pints?

Activity 24

This puzzle has much in common with Activity 12 and
Activity 35 and has been in circulation in some form since
the early part of this century. The solution here depends on

the fact that the canoe can hold two boys but it only needs one boy to take the canoe across the river. One boy paddles the canoe to the soldiers on the left bank. A soldier then paddles himself and his kit to the right bank where he stays. The second boy now paddles the boat to the left bank, collects the first boy and returns to the right bank. This process is repeated until each soldier has crossed the river.

Activity 25

The block moves forward 2 metres.

Although many shapes could be used as cross-sections of rollers only a circle would do for a wheel – unless you want a bumpy ride that is! To get the smoothest possible ride, the wheels' axle needs to be attached to the centres of the wheels. Of course, only circular wheels have a constant distance from axle to edge.

See also *Machines, Mechanisms and Mathematics* by A. B. Bolt and J. E. Hiscocks, and *Riddles in Mathematics* by E. P. Northrop.

Activity 26

The results here are always very surprising to the person meeting them for the first time. With a systematic approach it should be possible to find a pattern relating the number of twists in a band and the subsequent result of cutting down the middle. At one level this activity is enormous fun but it also has a serious side in posing questions about the nature of different surfaces. See for example *Mathematics and the Imagination* by E. Kasner and J. Newman, or *Experiments in Topology* by S. Barr.

Activity 27

A and *B* are inside and *C* is outside.

Every time the boundary is crossed you travel from inside to outside or vice versa.

Any circle around the ring would do or one like an equator for example. *Experiments in Topology* by S. Barr gives further ideas for anyone wanting to pursue this branch of mathematics. Also, *Mathematics and the Imagination* by E. Kasner and J. Newman has a readable section on this problem in the chapter headed 'Rubber-sheet Geometry'.

Activity 28

The paths will all be made up of arcs of circles as the packing case is always turning about one of the edges.

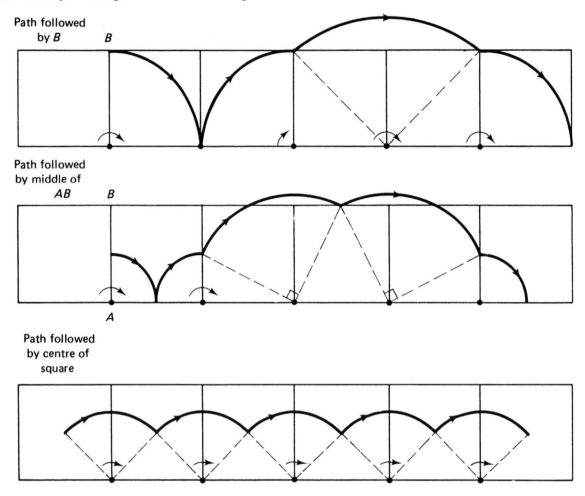

Path followed by B

Path followed by middle of AB

Path followed by centre of square

Activity 29

In each case the direction in which A, B, C and D move can be found by drawing a line (dotted here) from the point about which the wheel is turning, and then the arrow giving the direction of motion is at right-angles to this.

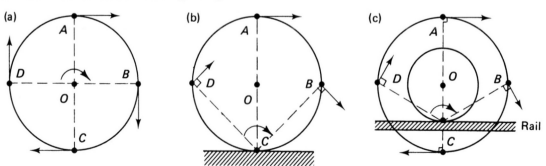

(a)

(b)

(c)

Rail

140

In (a) the wheel turns about its centre O.

In (b) the wheel turns about C, the point where it touches the ground.

In (c) the wheel turns about the point where it touches the rail.

A moves from left to right in each case but the directions in which B and D move vary considerably. Diagram (c) shows why it can always be said that part of an express train is travelling backwards – the faster the train is travelling forward, the faster will point C move backwards.

Activity 30

      (a) anticlockwise, 4 turns
      (b) clockwise, 1 turn
      (c) anticlockwise, 1 turn
      (d) clockwise, $\frac{1}{2}$ turn

Rule I   With an even number of rotating shafts the direction of the last shaft is always opposite to the direction in which the first shaft turns.

Rule II   When there is only one gear wheel on a shaft, as in (a), (b), (c) and (d), the angle through which B turns depends only on the number of teeth on A and on B:

$$\text{angle turned through by } B = \left(\frac{\text{number of teeth on } A}{\text{number of teeth on } B} \right) \text{ turns}$$

In (e), (f) and (g) the gear train needs to be broken down into parts to which the above rules apply.

(e) The second shaft makes 3 turns for each turn made by A. B makes 4 turns for each turn made by the second shaft. Thus B makes 12 turns (3 × 4) for each turn made by A. B also turns in the same direction as A as there are an odd number of shafts.

(f) The second shaft makes $\frac{1}{3}$ turn for each turn made by A. The third shaft makes $\frac{2}{3}$ turn for each full turn of the second shaft. B makes $\frac{1}{2}$ turn for each turn of the third shaft. Thus B makes $\frac{1}{3} \times \frac{2}{3} \times \frac{1}{2} = \frac{1}{9}$ turn for each full turn made by A. As there are an even number of shafts, B turns in the opposite direction to A.

(g) The second shaft makes 3 turns for each turn made by A. B makes $1\frac{1}{2}$ turns for each turn made by the second shaft. Thus B makes $4\frac{1}{2}$ turns (3 × $1\frac{1}{2}$) for each turn made by A. As there are an odd number of shafts, B turns in the same direction as A.

Sometimes gears are used to increase a turning speed as in a hand drill or egg whisk and in other mechanisms the gears slow down a turning speed such as in a clock, record turntable or food mixer.

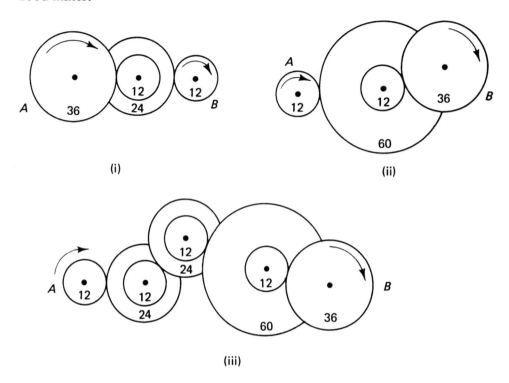

(i)

(ii)

(iii)

The direction of motion of the output shaft can be reversed in each case by introducing one more shaft into the train with a single wheel on it. The number of teeth on this additional wheel will not change the overall gear rate.

For more ideas on gear trains see *Machines, Mechanisms and Mathematics* by A. B. Bolt and J. E. Hiscocks.

Activity 32

Sixteen moves are required. They are best thought of as four groups of moves in which the four knights move from corner squares to middle squares, and vice versa in a kind of square dance in which they rotate as a foursome about the centre square. This puzzle has been known for a long time. The first record of it in Europe dates back to 1512.

   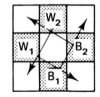

Activity 33

This is another shunting puzzle which became popular in the early part of this century. Like most of its kind it is tantalising because it is easy to state but until it has been solved the puzzler may well think it is unsolvable. It often helps to use some coloured bricks (e.g. multilink cubes) to represent the trucks and the engine.

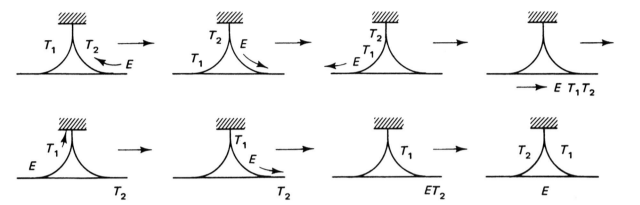

Activity 34

Paint each one centimetre cube in such a way that the three faces meeting at one corner are all red and the three faces meeting at the opposite corner are all blue. The eight cubes can then be fitted together to make either a red two-centimetre cube or a blue two-centimetre cube.

The three-centimetre cube is a much harder problem and it might require a visual aid – try colouring sugar lumps. The colouring is possible. The 27 one-centimetre cubes have 27×6 square faces while the three three-centimetre cubes have 3×6 faces each made of nine squares. Thus there are just the right number of squares to go round if they can be correctly coloured.

In a red three-centimetre cube the smaller cubes appear in four distinct ways.

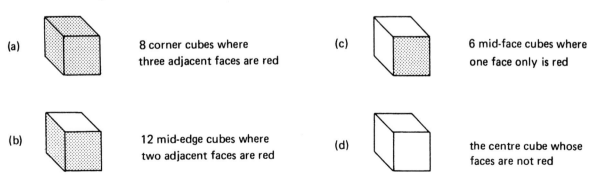

(a) 8 corner cubes where three adjacent faces are red

(c) 6 mid-face cubes where one face only is red

(b) 12 mid-edge cubes where two adjacent faces are red

(d) the centre cube whose faces are not red

There must be the same numbers of blue cubes and yellow cubes for a solution to exist and considerations like this lead to the following solution:

6 cubes coloured $R_2B_2Y_2$
3 cubes coloured $R_3B_2Y_1$ The letter indicates the colour
3 cubes coloured $R_3B_1Y_2$ and the suffix the number of
3 cubes coloured $R_2B_3Y_1$ faces of that colour. Where
3 cubes coloured $R_1B_3Y_2$ there are two or three faces
3 cubes coloured $R_2B_1Y_3$ of the same colour they are
3 cubes coloured $R_1B_2Y_3$ always next to each other.
1 cube each
coloured R_3B_3 B_3Y_3 Y_3R_3

The notation has been invented for the problem and is very helpful in describing the different cubes. This is a typical device used by mathematicians who will use letters and symbols to suit the problem in hand rather than many words.

Activity 35

As with the previous puzzle it is helpful to develop some kind of notation to describe the situation. Here the couples are denoted by Aa, Bb, Cc etc., where the capital letter stands for the husband and the small letter for his wife.

With three couples the boat will need to be rowed across the water five times. One solution is given below:

	abc →	← a	ABC →	← A	Aa →
Aa	A | a	Aa	a | A	Aa	| Aa
Bb	B | b	B | b	| Bb	| Bb	| Bb
Cc	C | c	C | c	| Cc	| Cc	| Cc
	1	2	3	4	5

First the three wives abc row across and then wife a rows the boat back. Next the three husbands ABC row to safety leaving wife a at the hotel and finally husband A returns to rescue his courageous wife!

You may find this puzzle easier to solve by using labelled pieces of paper to represent the people.

The following solution with five couples satisfies all the conditions but it takes thirteen crossings and you may find a better one. If you do the author would like to hear from you.

$\overset{abc}{\rightarrow}$ $\overset{}{\leftarrow} a$	$\overset{Aa}{\rightarrow}$ $\overset{}{\leftarrow} A$	$\overset{ABC}{\rightarrow}$ $\overset{}{\leftarrow} Aa$	$\overset{ADE}{\rightarrow}$	$\overset{A}{\leftarrow}$ $\overset{}{\rightarrow} Aa$	$\overset{D}{\leftarrow}$ $\overset{}{\rightarrow} Dd$	$\overset{E}{\leftarrow}$ $\overset{}{\rightarrow} Ee$

Aa	Aa		A	a	Aa		a	A	Aa	Aa	Aa
Bb	B	b	B	b	Bb	Bb	Bb	Bb	Bb
Cc	C	c	C	c	Cc	Cc	Cc	Cc	Cc
Dd	Dd		Dd	Dd	d	D	d	D		Dd	Dd
Ee	Ee		Ee	Ee	e	E	e	E	e	E	Ee

First the three wives *abc* row across and wife *a* returns with the boat. Then *A* and his wife row across, his wife gets out and *A* returns the boat. (NB *A* does not get out of the boat or he would be on the bank with *b* and *c* when their husbands were not present.) Now *ABC* row across and *Aa* row back leaving couples *Bb* and *Cc* in safety. The three husbands *ADE* now row across leaving their three wives *ade* temporarily at the hotel. *A* returns to pick up his wife then *D* and *E* follow suit.

Activity 36

This is a new version of another traditional puzzle. If you imagine the room rather like a shoe box and you open it up to form its net then the shortest distance from *A* to *B* is a route across the floor, a side wall and the ceiling whose length is 40 ft.

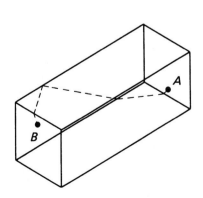

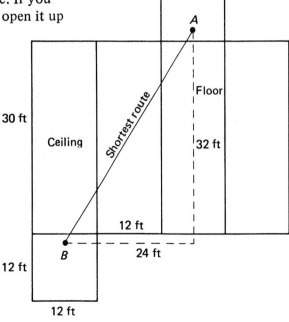

145

Activity 37

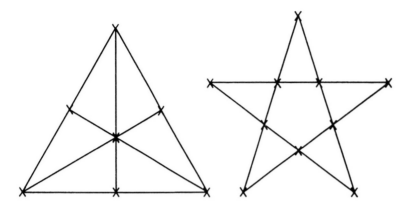

Activity 38

You will probably find that, to start with, this activity is tackled in a rather hit or miss fashion but then patterns of thought begin to emerge and the approach becomes systematic.

One particularly helpful approach is to take a 3 × 3 square or a 4 × 2 rectangle as a starting point and then imagine ways in which the boundary could be turned in as illustrated in (a).

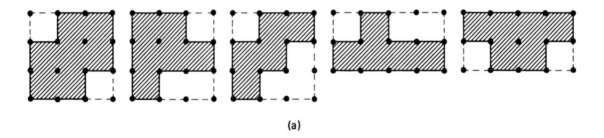

(a)

There is only one solution based on a 5 × 1 rectangle and a limited number based on the 4 × 2 rectangle. Most of the shapes come from the 3 × 3 square. This activity shows clearly that shapes having the same perimeter do not necessarily have the same area.

The fact that a triangle with sides of 3, 4 and 5 units is right-angled, extends the number of shapes with a perimeter of 12 in an interesting way. Some of the possible shapes are shown in (b).

(b)
5
3
4

The total number of possible shapes with a perimeter of 12 which can be found depends on the kind of shape which is allowed. If lines can cross over then many additional shapes can be found whilst if the lines can double back on themselves the total becomes very large. With a group working on this activity it has always been interesting to see just what shapes are seen as acceptable and leads to a discussion for the need of a precise definition of 'a shape with a perimeter of 12 units which can be made on a pinboard'. Which of the shapes in (c) do you find acceptable?

(c)

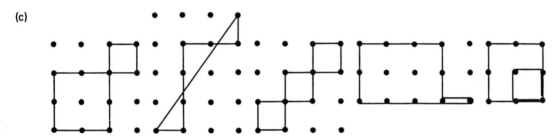

Activities 39 and 40

Repeating patterns are very common with man-made objects. The way bricks are laid in a wall, roofs tiled, paving slabs laid, carpets and wallpapers manufactured – all correspond to tessellations because of the way a basic unit is repeated again and again.

It is interesting to realise that any shape of quadrilateral can be used as the basic unit for a tessellation. Cut out a quadrilateral from a piece of card to use as a template which you can draw around. Start with one quadrilateral (shaded) and draw in the others by rotating the quadrilateral through 180° about the middle point of each side in turn.

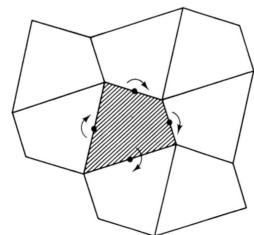

Over the years many interesting tessellations have been published in magazines such as *Mathematics Teaching* and *Mathematical Pie*. However for anyone with an interest in the links with art the book *The Graphic Work of M.C. Escher* is a must. A scientific link is found in *The Third Dimension in Chemistry* by A. F. Wells.

Activity 41

Measuring the area of a shape is closely related to covering the shape with a tessellation of a basic shape corresponding to the unit of area. The basic shape is usually taken as a square. In this activity the idea is to keep the area constant (2 square units) and see what a large variety of different shapes can be found even with the restriction of having the vertices confined to the points of a 3 x 3 pinboard. The key to finding new shapes is to see right-angled triangles as having half the area of a rectangle, as for example in (a), (b) and (c). These triangles can then be fitted together in a large variety of ways to generate shapes with an area of 2 square units.

The area of a shape may be seen in two ways and both should be explored:

(i) as the sum of smaller shapes,
(ii) as what is left when pieces are cut off a larger shape.

For example, the shaded shape shown in (d) could be seen (i) as the sum of a unit square and two triangles each of which is half a unit square or (ii) as a larger square of 4 units minus a unit square and two triangles each of half a unit square.

This activity is much more fundamental and significant than the usual text-book exercises of finding areas of rectangles using length multiplied by breadth.

With a 5 x 5 pinboard many more shapes can be found because triangles such as the following are now possible.

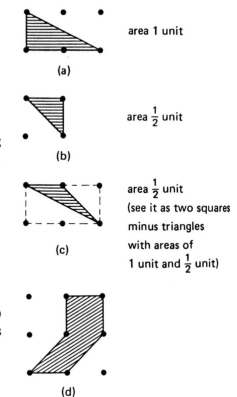

(a) area 1 unit

(b) area $\frac{1}{2}$ unit

(c) area $\frac{1}{2}$ unit (see it as two squares minus triangles with areas of 1 unit and $\frac{1}{2}$ unit)

(d)

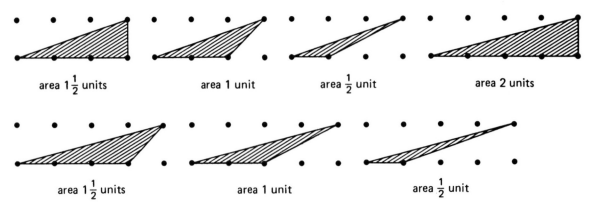

area $1\frac{1}{2}$ units   area 1 unit   area $\frac{1}{2}$ unit   area 2 units

area $1\frac{1}{2}$ units   area 1 unit   area $\frac{1}{2}$ unit

Activity 42

Before doing this activity you need to be confident that you can correctly deduce the areas of the shapes you make.

For all the shapes with only 1 interior pin it is true that

$$A = \tfrac{1}{2} b$$

that is, the area is exactly half the number of pins on the boundary of the shape.

For all the shapes with 12 boundary pins it is true that

$$A = i + 5$$

that is, the area is equal to the number of interior pins plus 5.

These results are special cases of the more general result known as the Pict's theorem that

$$A = i + \tfrac{1}{2} b - 1.$$

Activity 43

All routes must be of length 24 as there are 25 pins to be visited so there are 24 steps between them. In general the length is $n^2 - 1$. Routes with rotational symmetry are possible – try making up routes by starting from each end and meeting in the middle.

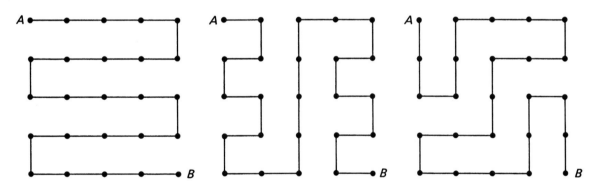

On a 3 x 3 board when diagonal routes are allowed then there are many possibilities. Because there are 9 pins then 8 steps will always be required to get from A to B. To find the shortest route all these steps will need to be across or up and down but to find the longest route it is necessary to use as many diagonal steps as possible.

The shortest route is 8 units long where a unit is the distance from one pin across the board to the nearest pin.

On a 3 × 3 board only two kinds of diagonal steps are possible as shown here. A step like PQ is of length $\sqrt{5}$ which is approximately 2·236 units, while a step like QR is of length $\sqrt{2}$ which is approximately 1·414 units.

These results can be deduced from Pythagoras' theorem for right-angled triangles or by scale drawing. In the latter approach the same accuracy cannot be expected. When the route cannot cross itself then the longest route is shown in (a) and its length is approximately 12·13, but when the route can cross itself more steps like PQ can be used and the longest route is shown in (b) with approximate length 15·42. Notice the symmetry in both solutions.

(a) A

$$AB = 1 + \sqrt{2} + \sqrt{5} + \sqrt{2} + \sqrt{2} + \sqrt{5} + \sqrt{2} + 1$$
$$\simeq 12\cdot13$$

(b) A

$$AB = \sqrt{5} + \sqrt{5} + \sqrt{5} + 1 + 1 + \sqrt{5} + \sqrt{5} + \sqrt{5}$$
$$\simeq 15\cdot42$$

One solution which might look better than the above because it does not contain any short steps is shown in (c), but its length is equivalent to $4\sqrt{5} + 4\sqrt{2} \simeq 14\cdot6$

(c) A 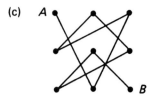 B

Activity 45

There are two stages to solving this puzzle. The first is to determine the different kinds of triangle which can be made and then how many of each kind.

150

These diagrams show the eight kinds of triangle which can be formed on a 3 × 3 pinboard.

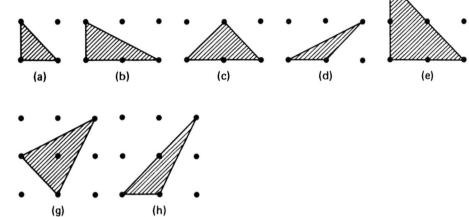

(a)   (b)   (c)   (d)   (e)   (f)

(g)   (h)

It should not be too difficult to see now that there are

16 of type (a)   as four to each square of pins and four squares
16 of type (b)   as two to each pair of pins on the edge of the board
 8 of type (c)   one to each side, four pointing to the centre
16 of type (d)   two to each corner, two to each mid-point of side
 4 of type (e)   as one to each corner of board
 4 of type (f)   as one to each side of board
 4 of type (g)   as one to each corner of board
 8 of type (h)   as two to each edge of board

A total of 76 different triangles can be made.

Activity 46

It will probably help to label all the points where lines intersect with letters and then label the triangles using the letters. Although this puzzle may appear to have much in common with the previous one it requires a different approach. First record, for example, all the triangles which have AB as a side, then AC etc.

ABE	ABG	ABH	ABI
ACD	ACE	ACG	ACI
ADE	AEI	AGH	AGI
BCE	BCF	BCG	BCI
BEF	BEG	BGI	BHI
CDI	CEG	CEI	CFG
DEI	DFH	EFG	EGI
GHI			

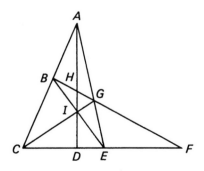

By keeping the letters in alphabetic order it is easy to spot whether you have counted a triangle twice.

Activity 47

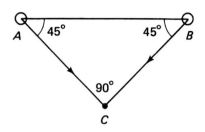

This is an interesting puzzle and might at first seem impossible.

No matter what path the boats follow they will not come together until the controller steers the boat to the point C shown in the above diagram. At this point the distance AC is equal to the distance BC and the bearing of C from B is $90°$ more than the bearing of C from A. When the boat from A reaches C by whatever path the boat from B will be there also.

Activity 48

$$A \to C \to E \to B \to D \to A \to B \to C \to D \to E \to A$$

There are many other possible solutions such as

$$A \to B \to C \to D \to A \to C \to E \to B \to D \to E \to A$$

A network is traversible if it can be drawn without taking the pencil off the paper or having to go over any line twice. The first network here is thus said to be traversible but the second one can only be drawn in four parts so the pencil has to be taken off the paper three times.

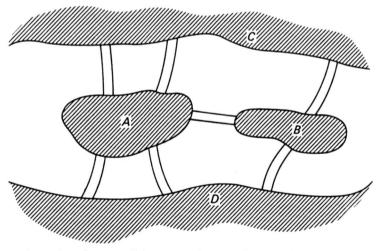

A study of traversible networks was first made by the mathematician Euler in the early part of the eighteenth century when he studied the now famous problem of the Königsberg bridges. Königsberg was a German town built on two islands and the banks of the River Pregel. The islands and river banks were connected by seven bridges as shown and the citizens of the town had, for many years, tried to find a way of starting from one point in the town, crossing every bridge once and then returning to their starting point. They could not find a way and when Euler became aware of the problem he was able to prove conclusively that the problem was incapable of solution. He first replaced the above map by a network which retained the significant features of the map where each region of the town was reduced to a point and the bridges by arcs. The problem now reduces to showing that this network cannot be drawn without taking your pencil from the paper.

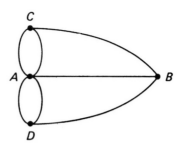

Euler realised that the key to the problem lay in the fact that the number of arcs meeting at A, B, C and D was odd – 3 at B, C and D, and 5 at A.

He showed that a point of a network with an odd number of arcs meeting at it (an odd node) could only be a starting point or a finishing point to trace the network, so the Königsberg problem which has 4 odd nodes cannot be solved.

To see why an odd node cannot be an intermediate point in a traversible network consider the 3-node P shown here with branches labelled 1, 2 and 3. In tracing a network in which P occurs let the first time the pencil comes to P be along 1. It can then leave via 2 say and at some stage it must return along 3, but then there is no route left to leave P which has not already been traced. Similar arguments can be used for any odd node and it follows that an odd node can only be used as a starting point or a finishing point. From this it can be shown that a network is only traversible if (i) all its nodes are even (i.e. have an even number of arcs meeting at them) or (ii) all its nodes are even except two which are odd and then they must be the starting point and the finishing point. The town of Königsberg could thus solve its problem by blowing up bridge AB for example or adding a second bridge from A to B. A good reference on this and related problems is *Mathematical Recreations and Essays* by W. W. Rouse Ball.

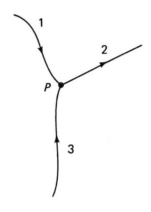

Activity 49

One solution of the knight's problem is shown here. Check yourself to see how each square is attacked.

There are analogous problems with the other chess pieces. For example, it can be achieved with five queens or nine kings or eight bishops. Have a go!

Activity 50

To handle this puzzle efficiently it is again necessary to
develop some means of recording the moves made. It is also
helpful to mark out the railway network on a larger scale and
use some numbered counters to represent the trains. The
following solution takes fifteen moves which are indicated by
the arrows.

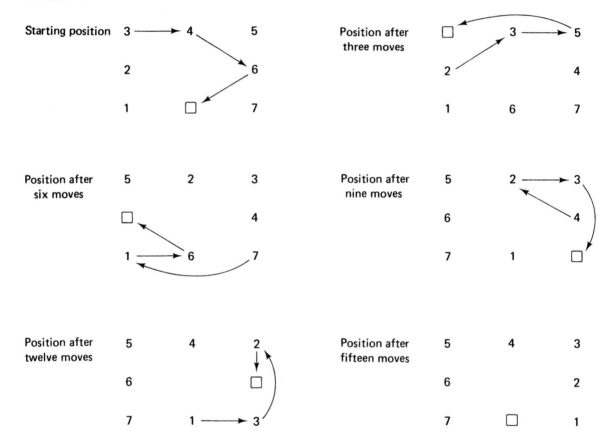

Activities 51 to 55 – general comments

These activities are all concerned with developing a better
understanding of how moving shapes interact with each other.
Much of the geometry traditionally taught in schools has
grown out of land surveying and little has been done to make
people aware of the geometry of motion. The ideas here have
grown out of the author's concern to make geometry more
relevant to our everyday experiences and have been explored
further in the book *Machines, Mechanisms and Mathematics*.
To get the most from these activities it is essential to
construct models using materials such as geostrips and
Meccano, but thick card strips are quite satisfactory.

Activity 51

'*AB* moves to and fro' is the usual description. The path traced by *A* is part of a circle whose centre is at *D* and with radius *DA*. Every other point of *AB* traces out a similar part of a circle with centre on *DC*.

BC always turns through the same angle as *AD*, in this case 30°.

The windscreen wiper probably sweeps out a better shape but the most likely reason is that the blade pushes the water to one side more efficiently than the usual car wiper which spends half its time pushing water up the windscreen where it can run down again.

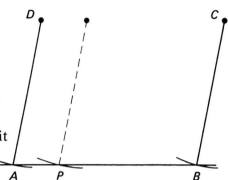

Activities 52 and 53

It is interesting to note that the modern Tom Cobley rocking horse uses essentially the same linkage as some Victorian rocking horses. This same linkage is also to be found at the centre of a seesaw in some modern children's playgrounds but it is not clear what advantage this has over a simple pivot.

The models of the Tom Cobley or the car's steering mechanism are instructive tc make and worth the time and effort taken–buy yourself a box of paper fasteners!

Activity 54

Watt's parallel motion linkage traces out a path rather like a tall, thin figure of eight while Tchebycheff's linkage traces out a path rather like a squashed semicircle. These are best seen by making models for yourself.

Activity 55

This is not unlike the pantograph which is available in many toy shops as an instrument for enlarging a figure. The combination of two simple linkages to make one which produces a translation is fascinating to observe in operation.

Activity 57

Not only are the four pieces identical to each other, but they are the same shape as the original.

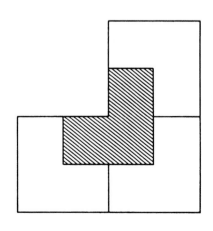

Activity 58

This puzzle is now available commercially in a variety of
packs made of plastic pieces but you could easily make
your own from coloured card.

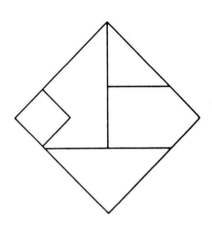

Activity 59

A makes two revolutions. The queen's head will be upside
down when penny *A* has rolled to the top of penny *B*, the
correct way up when *A* is to the right of *B*, upside down
when *A* is below *B* and the correct way when *A* is back at
the start.

Activity 60

A polar bear!
   One solution starts at the north pole see (a), but there are
infinitely many possibilities near the south pole. For example,
the hunter could start anywhere 3 miles north of the line of
latitude which is 3 miles in circumference, see (b), . . . or
3 miles north of the line of latitude which is $1\frac{1}{2}$ miles in
circumference . . . or etc.

(a)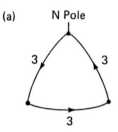

(b)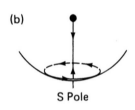

Activity 61

It is surprising that there are six arrangements in all, and you
may well have given up before turning to the solutions shown
here.

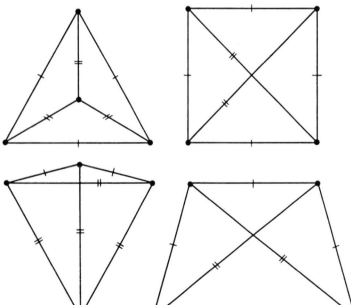

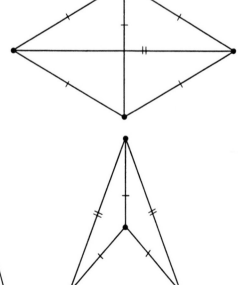

Activity 62

There must be a letter S opposite H. The arrangement of letters is shown in the net for the cube where it can be seen that there are in fact two letters S.

Activity 63

This is always successful, but take care to number the triangles exactly as shown and follow the folding instructions carefully. Do not use thick card or you will find it difficult to fold. To make a larger hexaflexagon it may be easier to cut out separate triangles and hinge them together using sellotape.

For more ideas on hexaflexagons read *Mathematical Puzzles and Diversions* by Martin Gardner.

Activity 64

This is a nice demonstration of Pythagoras' theorem. It neatly shows the equivalence of the areas of the two smaller squares to that of the square on the hypotenuse (the side of the triangle opposite to the right-angle).

Show also how pieces 1, 2, 3 and 4 can be fitted together to form a parallelogram.

Activity 65

This is not as easy as it looks to someone who has never met it before. The author has known people who have even made the half-tetrahedron shapes correctly but still been unable to put them together to make the whole tetrahedron. Faced with the two half pieces there is a great temptation to keep the long edges parallel.

Activities 67 and 68

These have been included after experience shows that ruler and compass constructions are rarely taught in school now although they are found stimulating and satisfying by many students of all ages.

The first activity gives some of the basic ruler and compass constructions and the second shows their use in constructing some of the circles associated with a triangle.

A related activity is to construct angle bisectors etc. using only the two sides of a ruler to obtain a pair of parallel lines a fixed distance apart. With this approach many of the traditional constructions can be achieved without a compass. See, for example, the appendix of School Mathematics Project, *Book T*, published by Cambridge University Press.

Activity 69

Designing games can be very rewarding.

Activity 70

The only two other fundamentally different solutions for the 4 × 4 board are shown here.

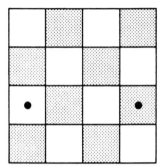 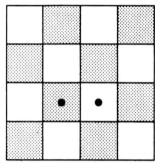

4 × 4 solutions

For a 5 × 5 board there are many solutions each requiring three queens. There are two more shown below. How many distinct solutions did you find?

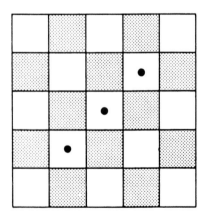 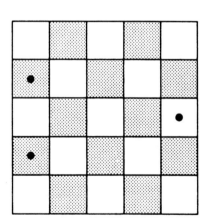

The 6 × 6 board can be solved with three queens too but in essentially only one way, while the 7 × 7 board requires four queens for its solution.

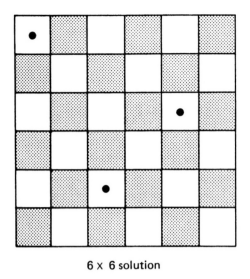

6 x 6 solution

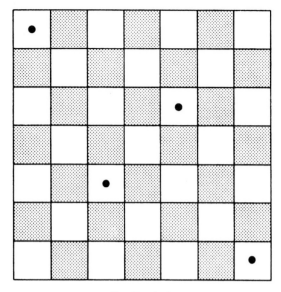

7 x 7 solution

With an 8 × 8 board the solution requires five queens and the solution given here also satisfies Jaenisch's further condition that no queen shall be under attack by another.

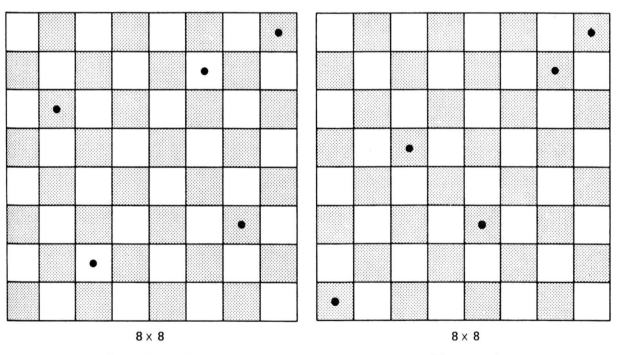

8 × 8

Not under attack

8 × 8

All supported

A good reference for further details on associated puzzles is *Mathematical Recreations and Essays* by W. W. Rouse Ball.

Activity 71

This is an old chestnut! The catch is that what looks like a diagonal of the 13 × 5 rectangle is in fact a very thin parallelogram whose area is 1 square unit.

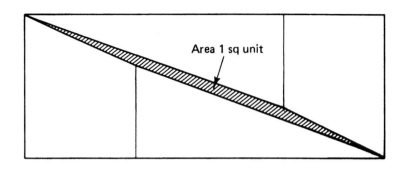

Area 1 sq unit

Activity 72

A, C, E, G, H and *I* are odd nodes and because of this one of the roads to each of them will have to be driven over twice. (See the comments on Activity 48.) To minimise the total distance to be covered the roads to be driven over twice can be arranged to be *AG, HC* and *IE*. One possible route is as follows:

$$A \rightarrow B \rightarrow C \rightarrow D \rightarrow E \rightarrow F \rightarrow A \rightarrow G \rightarrow F \rightarrow I \rightarrow E \rightarrow I \rightarrow D \rightarrow H \rightarrow C \rightarrow H \rightarrow B \rightarrow G \rightarrow H \rightarrow I \rightarrow G \rightarrow A$$

with a total distance of

$$(6 \times 13) + (9 \times 12) + (6 \times 5) = 216 \text{ miles}$$

Activity 73

It is impossible!

Imagine the domino painted half black and half white to match the chessboard squares. When two opposite squares of the board are removed the board loses two squares of the same colour. In the diagram given it is left with 30 black and 32 white squares so there is no way in which the dominoes can be placed to cover the board as each addition adds one black and one white square.

Activity 74

This is easy when you know how!

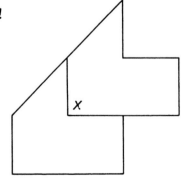

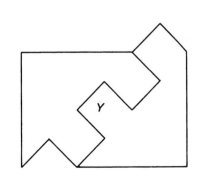

Activity 75

Experience shows that students enjoy the challenge of trying to find a map which cannot be coloured in fewer than five colours and often think they have succeeded until someone else shows how to re-colour it with four colours. The diagram here shows how the given map can be coloured using only four colours.

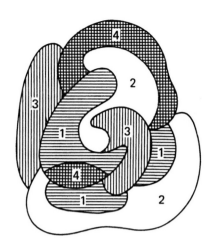

Interestingly on the surface of a torus (like a beach ring) it is possible to draw a map which cannot be coloured in less than seven colours. See, for example, *What is Mathematics?* by R. Courant and H. Robbins or *Riddles in Mathematics* by E. P. Northrop.

Activity 76

If you enjoy jigsaws this should keep you happy! The solutions given here were found by an 11 year old boy who, over a period of a few weeks, filled an exercise book full with different solutions. You can also find ways of forming other shapes such as a 5 × 5 square, for example, using a subset of pentominoes. You will often find the pentominoes and the hexominoes of the next activity produced commercially in plastic or wood but using coloured card is perfectly satisfactory.

An excellent reference for this activity and the next one is *Polyominoes* by Solomon W. Golomb.

All the pentominoes will tesselate.

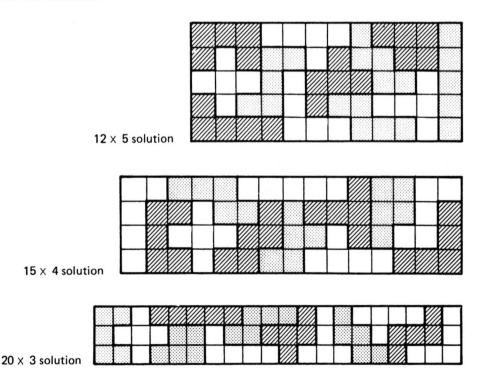

12 × 5 solution

15 × 4 solution

20 × 3 solution

The diagram below shows which of the pentominoes will form a net for an open box with its base shaded in each case.

See if you can find an arrangement of nine squares into which each of the twelve pentominoes can fit.

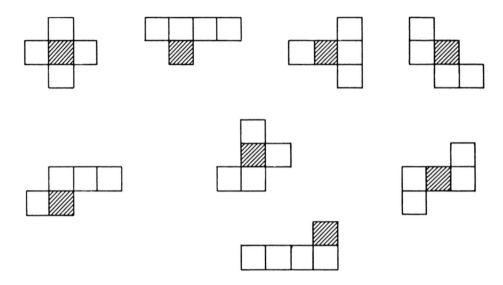

Activity 77

Here are the 35 distinct hexominoes. Those which can be folded to form a cube are shown shaded.

Note the systematic way in which the hexominoes are presented here. First the only one with a line of six squares then the three with a line of five squares. Next a line of four squares with two squares placed variously beneath them on both sides, etc.

There are only 11 *even* hexominoes and thus 24 *odd* hexominoes.

The 7 x 6 rectangle has 42 squares. Imagine this painted black and white as in a chessboard, then 21 of the squares will be black. Now seven *even* hexominoes will automatically have an even number of black squares on them altogether so could not equal 21.

A similar argument neatly shows why all 35 hexominoes could never be fitted together to form a rectangle. Such a rectangle would have 35 x 6 squares and thus 35 x 3 = 105 black squares. That is an *odd* number of black squares. Now the 11 *even* hexominoes must have an even number of black squares and so must the 24 *odd* hexominoes. Hence altogether the 35 hexominoes contain an *even* number of black squares. A rectangle is thus not possible.

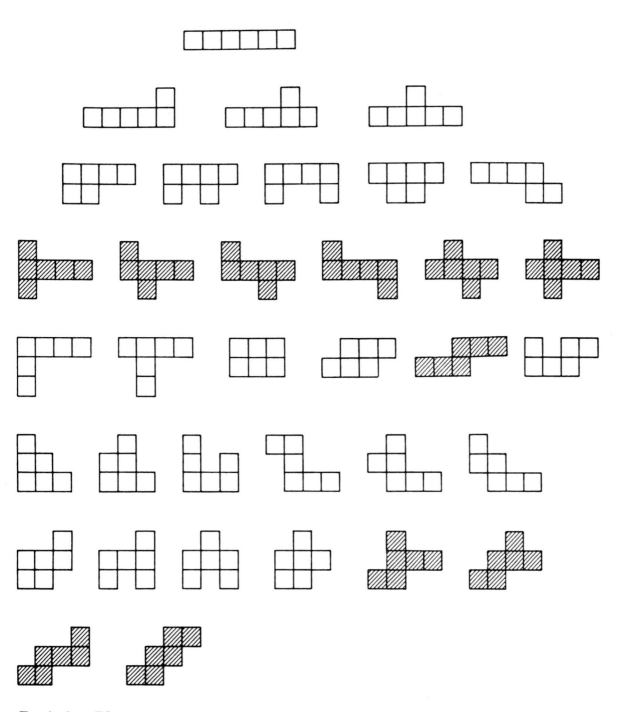

Activity 78

The other two half-cubes are shown in (a).

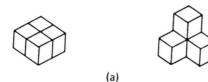

(a)

Other ways of dividing a 2 x 2 x 2 cube into two parts made up of unit cubes depends on the fact that eight cubes are involved, so the parts will be made from 7 + 1 or 6 + 2 or 5 + 3 or 4 + 4 unit cubes. The 4 + 4 situation has the three solutions already considered while the other situations each lead to only one solution (see (b), (c) and (d)).

(b) 7 + 1 solution   (c) 6 + 2 solution   (d) 5 + 3 solution

The best way to investigate new shapes is to make use of a set of cubes – sugar lumps can be quite useful if nothing else is available!

Shapes which can be made with five cubes are known as the pentacubes and there are 29 altogether. Twelve of these correspond to the pentominoes and are equivalent to placing a cube on each square of a pentominoe. This leaves seventeen genuinely three-dimensional shapes which are shown below. Many of these come in pairs which are mirror images but are such that they would not fit in the space left by their partner.

This activity invariably proves successful particularly when colourful multilink cubes are used to construct the shapes. A competitive element whereby two groups of people see who can find the largest number also adds interest. The opportunity can be used for exploring ways of recording shapes and the following examples show ways which have arisen in practice for the shape drawn on the left.

For further reading try *Polyominoes* by S. W. Golomb, or *More Mathematical Puzzles and Diversions* by M. Gardner, or *Creative Puzzles of the World* by P. Van Delft and J. Botermans.

Activity 79

This is an extension of the previous activity without the restriction of using unit cubes. However, the challenge here is to find ways of dividing a cube into two identical pieces. You may find modelling clay an aid to your investigation but models of your solutions can be made attractively in coloured card or wood.

Activity 80

You will need patience initially to cut out a good number of identical shapes but the rewards will be worthwhile. With the kit it is surprising how many solid shapes you discover which you would not have thought of without it. If you can persuade someone else to help make the triangles and squares etc. with you so much the better. This technique has the advantage that you need not buy expensive materials but make use of breakfast cereal packets for example. The author's kit was made ten years ago and is still usable.

Activity 81

The dodecahedron is a satisfying model to make. Take care to measure the 72° angles accurately when drawing the first pentagon in the circle, for errors at this stage will lead to an ill-fitting net later. It is not as difficult as you may first think and the stellated dodecahedron just requires the patience to add twelve pyramids, one to each face.

Activity 82

This game was designed by a group of students while learning about the transformations of reflection, rotation and translation. If you know what they are then you should enjoy matching your skill against your friends.

Activity 83

No matter how you try cutting up this cube there is no way of getting away from the fact that the one-centimetre cube in the centre has six faces all needing to be sawn, so the 27 cubes cannot be achieved with fewer than six saw cuts.

Activity 84

To show that it is possible to make a hole in a cube large enough to pass a larger cube through it, it is necessary to show that a cube has a cross-section larger than its square face. Consider the rectangle $ABCD$ shown in the diagram. A, B, C and D are each the same small distance from the corner of the cube to which they are nearest. AB is clearly longer than the edge PQ as it is at an angle to it. BC will be longer than an edge as it is almost equal to the diagonal QR. It would thus be possible to imagine a square hole cut through the cube of a larger size than the face of the original cube.

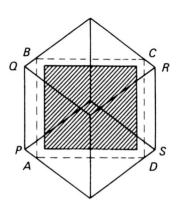

Activity 85

A neat way of seeing how to rearrange the pieces to form the 'square' is to imagine them hinged at P, Q and R and rotating them into the 'square' as shown here.

The 'square' is not exact, but a rectangle with sides in the ratio $7 : \sqrt{48}$. An exact solution is given by H. E. Dudeney in his book *The Canterbury Puzzles* (Dover).

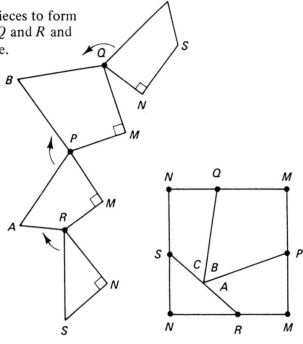

166

Activity 86

The key to this puzzle is in the pattern of circles from which the urn is composed.

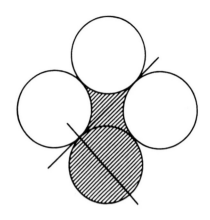

Activity 87

The apparent paradox is explained when Mrs Smith was shown a timetable which showed the times of the P buses and Q buses at her bus-stop.

P route	Q route
10.09	10.10
10.19	10.20
10.29	10.30
10.39	10.40
10.49	10.50
10.59	11.00

There is a gap of only one minute after a P bus visits the stop until a Q bus is due, but then a gap of nine minutes before the next P bus. Thus in any ten-minute period nine minutes could be spent waiting for a P bus but only one minute for a Q bus. The effect of this to a person using the bus stop frequently would be to find that in nine times out of ten a P bus would be the first to appear.

Activity 88

Three pennies need to be moved. Move the three corner pennies as shown.

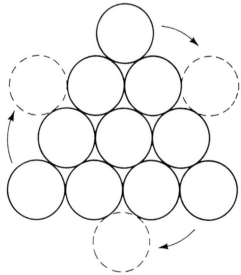

Activity 89

A knight's tour is impossible on a 4 x 4 board but it is
possible to find a path which visits fifteen squares. The
5 x 5, 6 x 6 and 7 x 7 tours are all possible, and a solution for
each is shown here.

6	9	2	15
1	12	5	8
10	7	14	3
13	4	11	

4 x 4 no solution

1	14	9	20	3
24	19	2	15	10
13	8	25	4	21
18	23	6	11	16
7	12	17	22	5

5 x 5 solution

11	22	33	44	13	24	3
32	43	12	23	2	45	14
21	10	39	34	37	4	25
42	31	36	1	40	15	46
9	20	41	38	35	26	5
30	49	18	7	28	47	16
19	8	29	48	17	6	27

7 x 7 solution

1	32	9	22	7	30
10	23	36	31	16	21
33	2	17	8	29	6
24	11	26	35	20	15
3	34	13	18	5	28
12	25	4	27	14	19

6 x 6 solution

You may find, like the author and many people before
him, that finding knight's tours becomes a fascination which
you can return to on and off over a lifetime!

Small rectangles on which a knight's tour is possible are a
5 x 4 and 4 x 3.

1	20	7	16	3
6	15	2	11	8
19	10	13	4	17
14	5	18	9	12

5 x 4 solution

1	4	7	10
8	11	2	5
3	6	9	12

4 x 3 solution

The solutions to the crosses are shown below with the second solution a re-entrant path.

		2	15		
		13	10		
12	1	16	3	14	9
17	6	11	8	19	4
		18	5		
		7	20		

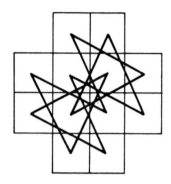

The solution of the 6 x 6 board shown above is a re-entrant path, due to the eighteenth century mathematician Euler, as the last square visited (36) is a knight's move from the first (1).

The reason a re-entrant path is not possible on a board with an odd number of squares depends on the fact that a knight's move always takes a knight to a square of a different colour. Suppose a tour starts on a black square then after an even number of moves it will have visited an odd number of squares and again be on a black square. This square, being the same colour as the starting square cannot be a knight's move from it.

A very good reference on this topic is *Mathematical Recreations and Essays*, by W. W. Rouse Ball.

Activity 90

We are used to thinking of distance as something we can measure with a ruler or tape measure but there are many situations where this may not be appropriate. If you live in a town with many one-way streets for example then the car distance between two points may be very different from the walking distance. The knight's move on a chessboard gives a particularly intriguing idea of distance.

Because of the way a knight always moves to a square of the opposite colour to the one it is on then it can only move from a white square to a white square by an even number of moves. Conversely any square which is an even number of moves from a white square must be white. The five unmarked white squares on the board given are each two moves from one of the squares labelled 2 and thus four moves from the knight.

The diagram on the left shows the distances of all the squares on a chessboard from a knight when it is placed in one corner. From this it can be seen that no square is ever more than six moves from a knight.

5	4	5	4	5	4	5	6
4	3	4	3	4	5	4	5
3	4	3	4	3	4	5	4
2	3	2	3	4	3	4	5
3	4	3	2	3	4	3	4
2	1	4	3	2	3	4	5
3	4	1	4	3	4	3	4
♘	3	2	3	2	3	4	5

Start

Activity 91

In reality skilled players can impart spin to a ball which can significantly change the way in which it bounces off a side cushion. Nevertheless the method described in this activity gives a good idea of the appropriate direction to hit the cue ball to get out of a snooker.

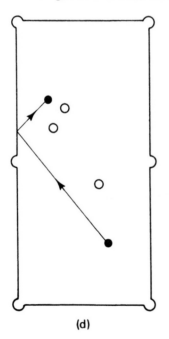

(d)

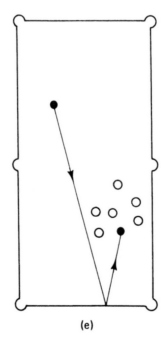

(e)

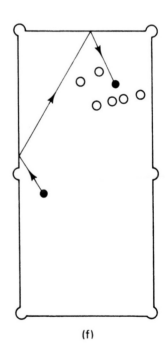

(f)

Activity 92

Euler's relation can be expressed symbolically as

$$V - E + F = 2$$

where V, E and F stand for the numbers of vertices, edges and faces of a polyhedron.

Polyhedra with holes through them do not satisfy the relationship and compare with disconnected networks. For further reading see, for example, *What is Mathematics?* by R. Courant and H. Robbins, or *Experiments in Topology* by S. Barr.

Activity 93

If you want to practice using your compass then you should find this a satisfying exercise. Start by drawing a line across the middle of your page and mark off $\frac{1}{2}$ cm intervals to help in getting the correct radius for the circles. The technique for using a compass efficiently is (i) make sure the arms are tight at the joint, (ii) arrange the pencil or ball point pen so that its tip meets the compass point when the arms are together, (iii) concentrate on applying pressure at the point of the compass, (iv) do not try moving the compass by holding the pencil.

Perhaps the most obvious family of curves other than ellipses is that of the hyperbolae.

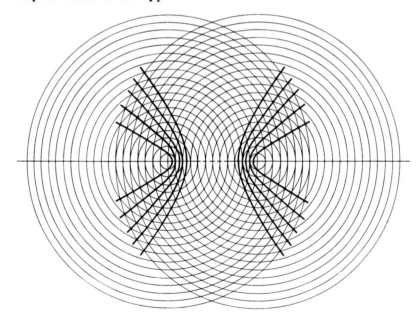

A good source book for other drawings of this kind is *A Book of Curves* by E. H. Lockwood.

Activity 94

Other ruled surfaces and models are described and illustrated
in books such as *Mathematical Models* by H. M. Cundy and
A. P. Rollett and *Mathematical Snapshots* by H. Steinhaus.

Activity 95

You need to be aware of
squares at an angle as well as
those the same way as the
board. See those in the diagram here for example.

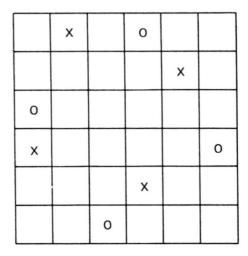

Activity 96

The answer is not 15 cm! The
diagram here represents the
view from the top of the books
and the dotted lines show the
bookworm's path which is
only 9 cm long!

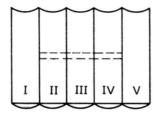

Activity 97

To solve this puzzle imagine
the motorway as the line of a
mirror and draw in the image
of Green Glades. Now join this
image to Pleasant Pastures by
a straight line and the point
where it crosses the motorway
is the position for *J*.

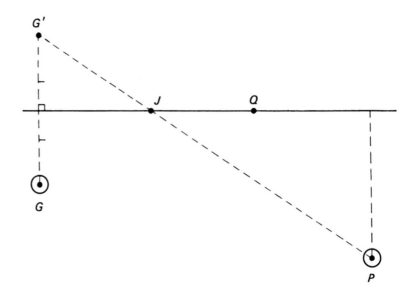

To see why this gives the shortest route note that

$$GJ + JP = G'J + JP = G'J$$

If Q is any other point on the motorway then

$$GQ + QP = G'Q + QP > G'P$$

as $G'QP$ is a triangle and two sides together must always be longer than the third side.

Activity 98

No matter how fast he goes down the hill he cannot average 40 km per hour. To do this he must cycle the 10 kilometres from A to C in a quarter of an hour, but he has already taken a quarter of an hour to climb up to B.

Activity 99

Contrary to what one might think the path is not a straight line from S to V. The path of quickest descent is in fact part of a cycloid and may even be uphill for part of its length. The cycloid is the path traced out by a point on the rim of a wheel as it rolls along a straight line.

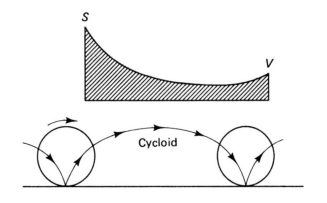

To draw a cycloid fasten to a desk a metre rule on top of a piece of paper. Roll a circular object (a tin lid, saucer) along the rule without slipping and trace out the path of a point on the object's edge. You can make a very effective demon-stration that this is the path of quickest descent by making two runners, one shaped like part of an inverted cycloid and the other a straight line, out of plywood or a plastic curtain runner down which you simul-taneously roll two marbles.

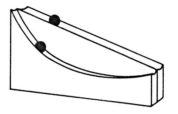

See also *Machines, Mechanisms and Mathematics* by A. B. Bolt and J. E. Hiscocks or *Riddles in Mathematics* by E. P. Northrop.

Activity 100

To make up your own puzzle start with a square and first see how to divide it into pentomines. Then letter it or put some motifs to suit.

E	A	I	O	I
U	E	U	E	O
O	I	A	O	A
I	U	E	A	I
A	O	U	E	U

Activity 101

The larger tetrahedron cannot be made from smaller ones. When you remove a tetrahedron from each corner of the large tetrahedron the shape left in the centre is an octahedron with a square cross-section which cannot be made up of the smaller tetrahedra.

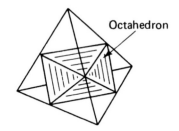

Octahedron

Activity 102

If h is the highest common factor of l and b then the relationship is

$$d = l + b - h$$

For example, if $l = 15$ and $b = 10$ then $h = 5$ so the number of squares crossed by a diagonal will be

$$15 + 10 - 5 = 20$$

Activity 103

No. of lines (n)	0	1	2	3	4	5	6	7
No. of regions (r)	1	2	4	7	11	16	22	29

Once the table has been completed it can be seen that the differences between the r numbers is 1, 2, 3, 4, 5, etc. from which it is not too difficult to deduce that for (i) when $n = 10$ then $r = 56$. The value for r when $n = 100$ (part (ii)) can be deduced in a similar way, but it is more easily calculated from the formula

$$r = 1 + \tfrac{1}{2}n(n + 1) \quad \text{as} \quad 5051.$$

Note that $\frac{1}{2} n(n+1)$ is the sum of all the numbers 1, 2, 3, ..., n which explains the formula for r. To see where $\frac{1}{2} n(n+1)$ comes from consider

$$S = 1 + 2 + 3 + 4 + \ldots + (n-1) + n$$
then $S = n + (n-1) + (n-2) + \ldots + 1$ by reversing the order

so $2S = (n+1) + (n+1) + (n+1) + \ldots + (n+1)$ by adding

$$= n(n+1)$$

from which $S = \frac{1}{2} n(n+1)$

The differencing technique which helps to extend a sequence of numbers is explored in the next activity and may help you when investigating the maximum number of regions (r) into which space can be divided by p planes.

No. of planes (p)	0	1	2	3	4
No. of regions (r)	1	2	4	8	15

After four planes it is difficult to visualise what is happening but the differencing technique suggests how it might continue.

```
                  1    2    4    8    15 /  26   42
                                      /
First difference      1    2    4    7 / 11   16
                                   /
Second difference       1    2    3 /  4    5
                                 /
```

Activity 104

The tenth term would be 120.

```
(i)    2    5    9    15    23   (33)

         2    4    6    8    10
```

```
(ii)   3    8    18    33    53   (78)

         5    10    15    20    25
```

(iii)   2   3   8   17   30   (47)

             1   5   9   13   17

(iv)   4   6   10   18   34   (66)

             2   4   8   16   32

The next two terms in the original sequence are 62 and 87,

(v) 67   (vi) 96   (vii) 238   (viii) 275

Activity 105

(i)   4   8   12   16   20   24   28   32   36   40
(ii) 1   5   13   25   41 . 61   85   113   145   181

The first sequence here forms the set of differences for the second sequence.

The hundredth number in sequence (i) is 400.
The hundredth number in sequence (ii) is equal to

$$
\begin{aligned}
&1 + \quad 4 + \quad 8 + 12 + 16 + \ldots + 396 \\
={}& 1 + 4(\ 1 + \ 2 + \ 3 + \ 4 + \ldots + \ 99) \\
={}& 1 + 2(\ 1 + \ 2 + \ 3 + \ldots + \ 97 + \ 98 + \ 99 \\
&\quad\quad + 99 + \ 98 + \ 97 + \ldots + \ 3 + \ 2 + \ 1) \\
={}& 1 \ + 2(100 + 100 + 100 + \ldots + 100 + 100 + 100) \\
={}& 1 \ + (2 \times 99 \times 100) \\
={}& 19\ 801
\end{aligned}
$$

The tenth triangle number can be easily found by differencing

1   3   6   10   15   21   28   36   45
   2   3   4   5   6   7   8   9

The sum of the first ten odd numbers is $10^2 = 100$.
The sum of the odd numbers $1, 3, 5, \ldots, 39$ is $20^2 = 400$ as 39 is the twentieth odd number.

The sum of the odd numbers between 60 and 100 is equal to the sum of the odd numbers from 1 to 99 minus the sum of the odd numbers from 1 to 59. Now 99 is the fiftieth odd number and 59 is the thirtieth so the required sum is $50^2 - 30^2$ = 1600.

Activity 106

Pinboard size	No. of squares
2 × 2	1
3 × 3	3
4 × 4	5
5 × 5	8
6 × 6	11
7 × 7	15
8 × 8	18

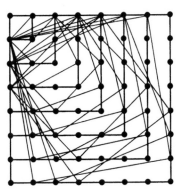

You may have thought that the number of different size squares on an 8 × 8 board was 19, but this overlooks the fact that one of the diagonal squares on an 8 × 8 board is based on a 3, 4, 5 triangle. The square thus has a side of length 5 and repeats the boundary square on a 6 × 6 board.

Up to this point the number of squares (N) can be expressed in terms of the number (n) of pins along one edge of a board by

$$N = \tfrac{1}{8} \left[2n^2 + 4n - 7 - (^-1)^n \right]$$

The areas of the squares which can be made on an 8 × 8 board are

1   2   4   5   8   9   10   13   16   17   18   20   25   26   29   36   37   49

Looking at the differences between them does not suggest any obvious pattern which would enable you to continue the number sequence.

Activity 107

(i) Triangle, quadrilateral, pentagon, hexagon.
Some others are: heptagon (7-sided), octagon (8-sided), nonagon (9-sided), decagon (10-sided).

(ii) 17 diagonals.

(iii) (a) 2   (b) 5   (c) 9
With n sides it is possible to draw $\tfrac{1}{2}n(n-3)$ diagonals. The reasoning behind this formula is that from any vertex it is possible to draw $(n-3)$ diagonals. There are n vertices so this gives $n(n-3)$ but as each diagonal is counted twice, as it originates from two vertices, this number must be halved.

(iv) (a) 2   (b) 3   (c) 4
In general $n-3$ diagonals can be drawn without any crossing for an n-sided polygon.

The diagrams (a) and (b) show two distinctly different ways in which the hexagon could be triangulated.

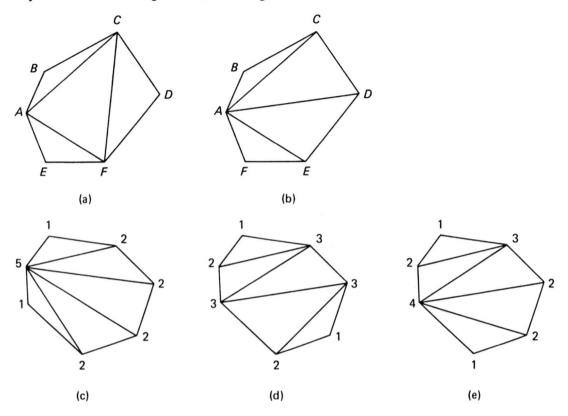

(a)   (b)

(c)   (d)   (e)

Diagrams (c), (d) and (e) show three further ways of triangulating the heptagon (7–gon).

$$1 + 5 + 1 + 2 + 2 + 2 + 2 = 15$$
$$1 + 2 + 3 + 2 + 1 + 3 + 3 = 15$$
$$1 + 2 + 4 + 1 + 2 + 2 + 3 = 15$$

In each case the triangulation of the heptagon produces five triangles. Each triangle occurs at three vertices so in the numbering system used each triangle is counted three times. Hence the same digit sum of $5 \times 3 = 15$ in each case.

Clearly the more sides a polygon has the greater the number of distinct triangulations. However the author has not yet found a way of predicting the number of distinct triangulations for a polygon with a given number of sides.

Apart from the problem of not knowing how many triangulations to expect one of the reasons to introduce this activity was to generate a sequence of numbers which would form the basis of a frieze pattern. These patterns were discovered relatively recently and are still little known. The arithmetic is very simple once you have mastered the way in which new lines are generated, and the patterns are intriguing.

178

Activity 108

Pegboard games are of long standing but perhaps underrated because they look deceptively simple.

The smallest number of moves in 'Leapfrog' is fifteen.

Number the holes 1 to 7 from left to right then a solution in fifteen moves is as follows where the number corresponds to the empty hole at each stage:

3   5   6   4   2   1   3   5   7   6   4   2   3   5   4

The strategy is to maximise the number of leaps and in this solution there are nine.

With x black pegs and y red pegs to change ends then the solution can be achieved in $xy + x + y$ moves where xy is the number of leaps.

The games described here and many others are analysed in *Mathematical Recreations and Essays* by W. W. Rouse Ball while readable references on solitaire problems are *Winning Ways* vol 2 by Berlekamp, Conway and Guy, and *Further Mathematical Diversions* by Martin Gardner.

Activity 109

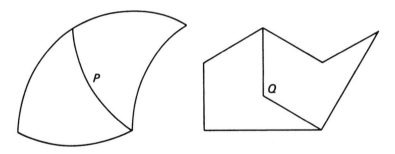

Activity 110

The smallest number of colours is three, as the three faces meeting at a corner of the cube all have to be different, but if opposite faces are the same colour then no adjacent faces are the same.

With four colours A, B, C and D available then there are four ways of choosing three at a time namely ABC, ABD, ACD and BCD and with each choice only one way of colouring the cube. All other ways must come from using all four colours. It is not easy to sort out the possibilities without a model cube (lumps of sugar can be very helpful here) but to start with note that three faces cannot be coloured the same colour without two adjacent faces being the same.

There are thus six faces to be coloured using all four colours which means that two colours must be used twice and two colours once each. This leads to the six solutions indicated by the nets shown here.

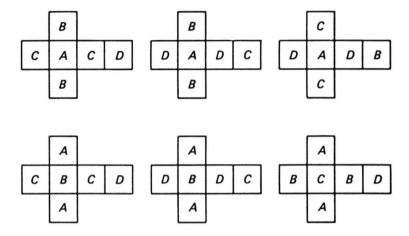

In each case the two colours which occur once must be on opposite faces.

These six solutions with the four earlier solutions using only three colours at a time give a total of ten distinct ways of colouring the cube.

Activity 111

The number sequence suggests 32 as the solution. In fact the answer is only 31. This is a good example to show that you cannot predict the next number of a sequence with any certainty unless you have more evidence.

For those who understand combinations, the number of pieces produced by n points is given by

$$^{n}C_4 + {}^{n}C_2 + 1$$

Activity 112

This is a good exercise for using a calculator. One approach is to form a table giving

$$n \quad n^2 \quad n^2 - 1 \quad \tfrac{1}{2}(n^2 - 1)$$

and a solution is found when a number in the $n^2 - 1$ column is repeated somewhere in the $\tfrac{1}{2}(n^2 - 1)$ column.

The solution to this puzzle is 840 as

$$840 + 1 = 841 = 29^2$$
$$\text{and } (840 \times 2) + 1 = 1681 = 41^2$$

Activity 113

As in the last puzzle you will need a table of square numbers.
The problem is to find whole number solutions to

$$a^2 + b^2 = c^2 + d^2$$

The first solution is

$$6^2 + 7^2 = 2^2 + 9^2 = 85$$

Other possible solutions are

$$8^2 + 11^2 = 4^2 + 13^2 = 185$$

and $15^2 + 20^2 = 7^2 + 24^2 = 625$

Activity 114

Solve these by intelligent use of 'trial and error'.

With $1, 2, 3, 4, 5, 6$, the four possibilities are

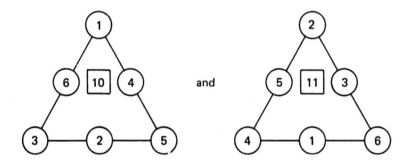

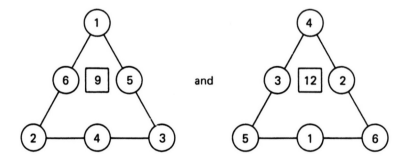

Notice how the solutions occur in pairs where the numbers
at the vertices of the triangles change places with the numbers
in the middle of the opposite sides.

With 1, 2, 3, 5, 6, 7 the solutions are

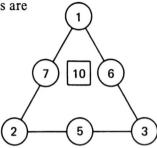 and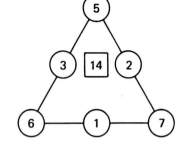

which are closely related to the last two above. How?

With 1, 2, 3, 4, 6, 7, the solutions are

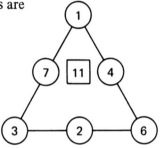 and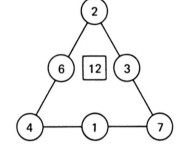

Activity 115

1 If the digit is *d* the answer is *ddd ddd ddd*. This is because
   12 345 679 = 111 111 111 ÷ 9.
2 If the digit is *d* the answer is *ddd ddd*. In this case 15 873
   = 111 111 ÷ 7
3 143 × 7 = 1001 so 143 × *d* × 7 = 1001 × *d* = *d*00*d*.
4 There are probably several logical explanations for each of
   these:

   (i) 1234 = 1111 + 111 + 11 + 1 + 0

   (1111 × 9) + 1 = 10 000
   (111 × 9) + 1 = 1 000
   (11 × 9) + 1 =   100
   (1 × 9) + 1 =   10
   (0 × 9) + 1 =   1

   (1234 × 9) + 5 = 11 111

   This example should show why the pattern occurs.

   (ii)
      66 × 67 = 2 × 3 × 11 × 67
             = 22 × 201
             = 4422

   666 × 67 = 2 × 3 × 111 × 67
           = 222 × 2001
           = 444222

   and so on.

Activity 116

The surprising fact is that no matter what four digits you start with the end point is 6174. Here is a longer chain.

(i)	7432	(ii)	8550	(iii)	9972	(iv)	7731
−	2347	−	558	−	2799	−	1377
	5085		7992		7173		6354

(v)	6543	(vi)	8730	(vii)	8532	(viii)	7641
−	3456	−	378	−	2358	−	1467
	3087		8352		6174		6174

The author has found chains of eight subtractions needed before 6174 occurs but he would be interested to hear from anyone who finds a longer chain.

This activity is best investigated with a calculator, it is a good idea to jot down the answer to your subtraction at each stage for if a long chain occurs you will have forgotten the starting point by the time 6174 occurs.

Try a similar process on five digits or longer numbers.

Activity 117

Put the digits in decreasing order:

$$9 \quad 7 \quad 5 \quad 4 \quad 3 \quad 2$$

Then for the largest sum it is only necessary to take the first two digits for the hundreds, the next two digits for the tens, and the last two digits for the units. This gives four possible pairs:

	953		943		952		942
+	742	+	752	+	743	+	753
	1 695		1 695		1 695		1 695

However the maximum product is found by taking the pair of numbers from the four here which are closest together, in this case

$$942 \times 753 = 709\ 326$$

One way to understand this is to imagine the four pairs above as representing the sides of a rectangle.

As the sum of each pair is the same the rectangles will all have the same perimeter. The products of the numbers then correspond to the areas of the rectangles and for rectangles of equal perimeter the shape nearest to a square will have the largest area.

Activity 118

One approach is to just add together and subtract different unit fractions to see what results. However, to make real progress certain patterns need to be recognised.

$\frac{1}{3} - \frac{1}{4} = \frac{1}{12}$ is a special case of $\dfrac{1}{n} - \dfrac{1}{n+1} = \dfrac{1}{n(n+1)}$

from which $\frac{1}{3} = \frac{1}{4} + \frac{1}{12}$

and hence $\frac{2}{3} = \frac{1}{3} + \frac{1}{12}$

This approach could be used for all fractions of the form $2/n$.

$\frac{3}{4}$ could have been written as $\frac{1}{2} + \frac{1}{4}$ or $1 - \frac{1}{4}$ but the example given illustrates an interesting pattern which may be better seen as

$$\frac{3}{4} = \frac{1}{4} + \frac{1}{5} + \frac{1}{6} + \frac{1}{4 \times 5} + \frac{1}{4 \times 6} + \frac{1}{5 \times 6} + \frac{1}{4 \times 5 \times 6}$$

which comes from

$$\left(1 + \tfrac{1}{4}\right)\left(1 + \tfrac{1}{5}\right)\left(1 + \tfrac{1}{6}\right) = \tfrac{5}{4} \times \tfrac{6}{5} \times \tfrac{7}{6} = \tfrac{7}{4} = 1 + \tfrac{3}{4}$$

similarly

$$\frac{3}{5} = \frac{1}{5} + \frac{1}{6} + \frac{1}{7} + \frac{1}{5 \times 6} + \frac{1}{5 \times 7} + \frac{1}{6 \times 7} + \frac{1}{5 \times 6 \times 7}$$

or $\frac{3}{5} = 1 - \frac{2}{5} = 1 - \frac{1}{5} - \frac{1}{6} - \frac{1}{30}$

Activity 119

This is an activity well worth spending time on. As a school activity it is interesting to put the results on the wall and encourage alternative expressions over a period of say a week. Numbers which prove difficult to express vary from person to person but there are one or two intrinsically difficult ones. Feel pleased if you find 95 or more correctly!

$$71 = \frac{4! + 4 \cdot 4}{\cdot 4} \qquad 73 = \frac{\sqrt[\cdot 4]{4} + \dot 4}{\dot 4} \qquad \left[\text{NB } \sqrt[\cdot 4]{4} = 4^{5/2} = 2^5 = 32 \right]$$

$$85 = \frac{4!}{\dot 4 \times \sqrt{\cdot 4}} + 4 \qquad 89 = \frac{4! + \sqrt{4}}{\cdot 4} + 4!$$

184

Activity 120

ShELL.OIL
    A calculator never tells LIES.
    LESLIE went fishing off LOOE on a LILO for SOLE but only caught some EELS.
    BILL decided to SELL hIS walking ShOES because hE had a LOOSE hEEL in one and a hOLE in the other. They hurt like hELL and made him feel quite ILL.
    ESSO.

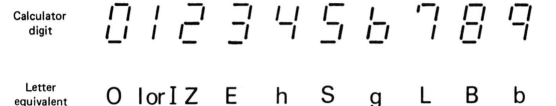

Calculator digit	0	1	2	3	4	5	6	7	8	9
Letter equivalent	O	I or I	Z	E	h	S	g	L	B	b

Activity 121

Because a calculator takes the drudgery out of arithmetic challenges like the ones here become relatively easy.

(i) 237×238 First find $\sqrt{(56\,406)}$.

(ii)   Intelligent use of trial and error should soon give
       $69 \times 71 \times 73 = 357\,406$

(iii) $26^2 + 27^2 = 1405$

(iv)   The intention here is to try different numbers and gradually get closer to the actual length.

       $5 \times 5 \times 5 = 125$ and $6 \times 6 \times 6 = 216$

       so the required length will be somewhere between 5 and 6 but nearer to 6.

Try	5·9	: $5{\cdot}9 \times 5{\cdot}9 \times 5{\cdot}9$	= 205·379
Next	5·8	: $5{\cdot}8 \times 5{\cdot}8 \times 5{\cdot}8$	= 195·112
	5·85	: $5{\cdot}85 \times 5{\cdot}85 \times 5{\cdot}85$	= 200·201 62
	5·845	: $5{\cdot}845^3$	= 199·688 72
	5·848	: $5{\cdot}848^3$	= 199·996 36
	5·848 1	: $5{\cdot}848\,1^3$	= 200·006 61
	5·848 04	: $5{\cdot}848\,04^3$	= 200·000 45
	5·848 035	: $5{\cdot}848\,035^3$	= 199·999 94

On a variety of calculators

   $5{\cdot}848\,035\,5^3 = 200$

This is not necessarily the *exact* answer, though within the accuracy of the calculator it is.

185

Activity 122

■	H	■	■	L	I	E
G	O	O	S	E	■	L
■	L	■	E	G	G	S
B	E	L	L	■	■	I
I	S	■	L	O	B	E
B	■	I	■	■	E	■
L	E	S	L	I	E	■
E	■	■	O	■	S	O

Activity 123

This is an interesting puzzle for a group of people to do together to see who can find the most profitable route. The idea for this came from an article in the *Mathematical Gazette* no. 418 and in turn came from a sales promotion gimmick by an Australian detergent manufacturer. It has proved particularly motivating in a competitive situation but so far no-one has found the best solution without using a computer. This is probably because the best route,

28 74 45 83 57 72 52 73 41 70 44 81 56

which gives a profit of £776 million, does not visit any of the eleven squares with profits of more than £83 million.

Using this array of numbers it is easy to pose similar but different puzzles. For example, what is the shortest route which would visit all the squares with a profit of at least £80 million?

Activity 124

The final answer is always 1089 unless the first number chosen has its hundred's digit equal to its unit's digit such as 525 for then the first subtraction yields zero.

Activity 125

The possible solutions all depend on the fact that $1+6 = 2+5 = 3+4 = 7$. In each case the pair of squares at the intersection of two circles must contain a pair of numbers which add up to 7. The magic number for each circle is then 14.

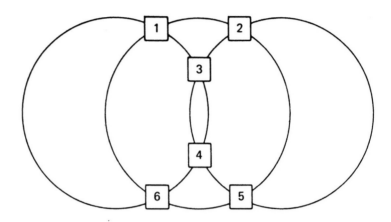

To find another set of six numbers which could be used to form a set of magic circles decide on a number N and find three pairs of numbers $(a, b), (c, d), (e, f)$ whose sum is N. For example, if $N = 15$, then the three pairs of numbers could be

$$(5, 10) \quad (7, 8) \quad (2, 13)$$

A solution would then be

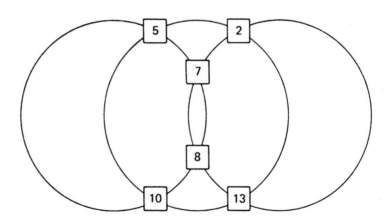

where $2N = 30$ is the magic number.

The solution to the four-circle puzzle depends on the fact that $1 + 12 = 2 + 11 = 3 + 10 = 4 + 9 = 5 + 8 = 6 + 7 = 13$.

Any pair of circles intersect in only two points so put a pair of numbers at these two points which add up to 13. In this way it is easy to find a solution. One is given here.

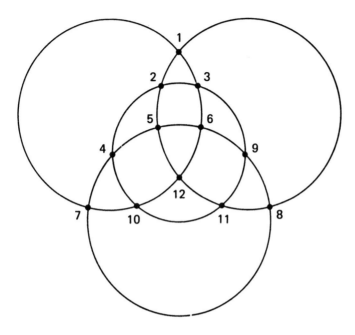

$$1 + 2 + 5 + 12 + 11 + 8 = 39$$
$$2 + 3 + 9 + 11 + 10 + 4 = 39$$
$$1 + 3 + 6 + 12 + 10 + 7 = 39$$
$$7 + 4 + 5 + 6 + 9 + 8 \quad = 39$$

Activity 126

The bottom spoke has all its numbers present and totals 23. The number in the centre can now be found as $23 - 15 - 2 = 6$ and the rest rapidly follow.

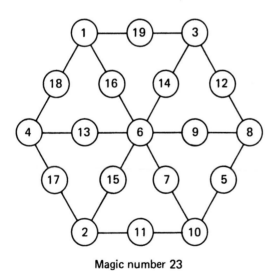

Magic number 23

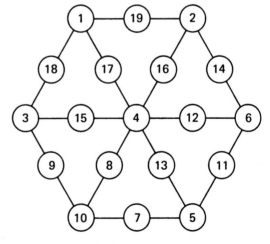

Magic number 22

Activity 127

Here are four solutions.

$$123 - 4 - 5 - 6 - 7 + 8 - 9 = 100$$

$$123 - 45 - 67 + 89 = 100$$

$$[1 \times (2+3) \times 4 \times 5] + 6 - 7 - 8 + 9 = 100$$

$$(1 \times 2 \times 3) - (4 \times 5) + (6 \times 7) + (8 \times 9) = 100$$

Activity 128

Because in the past without a calculator we usually only carried out a division process for say 4 significant figures it was only when dividing by numbers like 3 and 11 which give short repeating patterns that we were aware of the possibility of a recurring decimal. The fact that virtually all division sums if continued far enough lead to a repeating pattern probably comes as a surprise.

1 With division by 7 the pattern will always settle down to a recurring sequence of six digits.

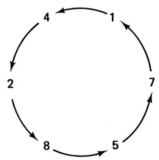

$$\tfrac{8}{7} = 1\tfrac{1}{7} = 1 \cdot 142857$$

$$\tfrac{9}{7} = 1\tfrac{2}{7} = 1 \cdot 285714$$

$$\tfrac{16}{7} = 2\tfrac{2}{7} = 2 \cdot 285714$$

$$\tfrac{1}{7} = 0 \cdot 142857\ 142857 \ldots$$

To see that division by a number such as 64 or 320 always terminates is probably best seen with an example.

Consider $\dfrac{73}{64} = \dfrac{73}{2^6} = \dfrac{73 \times 5^6}{2^6 \times 5^6} = \dfrac{1140625}{1000000} = 1 \cdot 140625$

If the number is not made up of a power of 2 and a power of 5 then it cannot be converted into a power of 10 as in the example here.

When dividing by a number such as 31, for example, then there are 30 possible remainders namely 1, 2, ..., 30 which could all occur before one is repeated so to study repeating sequences in the quotient it is really a case of studying the sequence of remainders. There is a nice tie-up here with modulo arithmetic groups for anyone interested.

2 For division by 17 the sequence of digits is

2 9 4 1 1 7 6 4 7 0 5 8 8 2 3 5

$$\frac{5}{17} = 0.294117647058823529 41$$

$$\frac{6}{17} = 0.3529411764705882 3529$$

$$\frac{7}{17} = 0.41176470588235294117$$

3 For division by 19 the sequence of digits is

3 6 8 4 2 1 0 5 2 6 3 1 5 7 8 9 4 7

4 Division by 11 always leads to a sequence of two digits which can be

09	18	27	36	45
90	81	72	63	54

5 Division by 13 leads to one of two six-digit sequences

0 7 6 9 2 3   or   1 5 3 8 4 6

Activity 129

29 and 31 are the only primes between 23 and 37.
127 is the next prime after 113.
There are four primes between 190 and 200 namely,
191, 193, 197 and 199.

1 28 = 5 + 23 = 11 + 17
    50 = 13 + 37 = 3 + 47
  100 = 3 + 97 = 29 + 71
  246 = 7 + 239 = 23 + 223

The representation is clearly not unique.

2   5 −   3 = 2
    11 −   7 = 4
    29 − 23 = 6
    97 − 89 = 8
  149 − 139 = 10
  211 − 199 = 12
  127 − 113 = 14

3 Here are the first ten odd numbers.

$$3 = 2 + 2^0$$
$$5 = 3 + 2^1$$
$$7 = 3 + 2^2 = 5 + 2^1$$
$$9 = 5 + 2^2 = 7 + 2^1$$
$$11 = 3 + 2^3 = 7 + 2^2$$
$$13 = 5 + 2^3 = 11 + 2^1$$
$$15 = 7 + 2^3 = 11 + 2^2 = 13 + 2^1$$
$$17 = 13 + 2^2$$
$$19 = 3 + 2^4 = 11 + 2^3 = 17 + 2^1$$
$$21 = 5 + 2^4 = 13 + 2^3 = 17 + 2^2 = 19 + 2^1$$

But try 1271.

4 179, 181; 191, 193; 197, 199

5 (ii) Write the numbers in six columns as follows.

1	2	3	4	5	6
7	8	9	10	11	12
13	14	15	16	17	18
19	20	21	22	23	24
.	.	.	.	.	.
.	.	.	.	.	.

The second, fourth and sixth columns are all even numbers so cannot be prime, except 2. The third column contains multiples of 3 so they are not prime except 3. This leaves the first column and the fifth column where the numbers are all of the form $6n + 1$ and $6n - 1$.

(iii) e.g.
$$5 = 2^2 + 1^2$$
$$13 = 3^2 + 2^2$$
$$17 = 4^2 + 1^2$$

In this activity and the next it may be advantageous to construct a table of primes. One neat way of doing this is to use the method due to Eratosthenes, an early Greek mathematician. Write down all the numbers you want to consider in some manageable array, say 1 to 50.

1	2	3	4̸	5	6̸	7	8̸	9̸	1̸0̸
11	1̸2̸	13	1̸4̸	1̸5̸	1̸6̸	17	1̸8̸	19	2̸0̸
2̸1̸	2̸2̸	23	2̸4̸	2̸5̸	2̸6̸	2̸7̸	2̸8̸	29	3̸0̸
31	3̸2̸	3̸3̸	3̸4̸	3̸5̸	3̸6̸	37	3̸8̸	3̸9̸	4̸0̸
41	4̸2̸	43	4̸4̸	4̸5̸	4̸6̸	47	4̸8̸	4̸9̸	5̸0̸

Now cross out every second number after 2. This leaves all the odd numbers and 2. Take the first number after 2 which is not crossed out, 3. Now cross out every third number after 3 such as 6, 9, 12 etc. Move to the next number from 3 which has not been crossed out, 5, and cross off every fifth number from it. Now cross off every seventh number from 7 etc. The numbers left are the primes.

This method has been described in detail in the School Mathematics Project *Book 1* and the associated teacher's guide but for further reading on prime numbers the following books are recommended: *What is Mathematics?* by R. Courant and H. Robbins, and *Recreations in the Theory of Numbers* by A. H. Beiler.

Activity 130

1 This first breaks down with the term $121 = 11^2$.

2 It breaks down when $n = 40, 41, 44, 49, 56, 65, 76$.
When $n = 40$, $n^2 + n + 41 = 40^2 + 40 + 41$
$$= 40 (40 + 1) + 41$$
$$= 40 (41) + 41$$
$$= 41^2$$

3 When $n = 80$, $n^2 - 79n + 1601 = 80^2 - (79 \times 80) + 1601$
$$= 80 (80 - 79) + 1601$$
$$= 1681$$
$$= 41^2$$

The two quadratics are very closely linked. Substituting $n - 40$ for n in $n^2 + n + 41$ gives $n^2 - 79n + 1681$.

4 $n = 29$, $2 \times 29^2 + 29 = 29 (58 + 1) = 29 \times 59$

5 The first five Fermat numbers are 3, 5, 17, 257 and 65 537.

Activity 131

Palindromic numbers

The smallest palindromic prime is 11 and the smallest palindromic square is 121. There are only two other palindromic squares less than 1000:

$$484 = 22^2 \quad \text{and} \quad 676 = 26^2$$

The palindromic primes between 100 and 200 are

$$101 \quad 131 \quad 151 \quad 181 \quad 191$$

Any palindromic number : between 400 and 500 would have to end in 4 so would be an even number; between 500 and 600 would have to end in 5 so would have 5 as a factor; between 600 and 700 would have to end in 6 so would be even. In fact there are no palindromic primes between 383 and 727. The common factor is 11.

Excessive, perfect and defective numbers

(i) Excessive: 1 2 3 4 5 7 8 9 10 11 13
              14 15 16 17 19 21 22 23 25
              26 27 29
   Defective: 12 18 20 24
   Perfect: 6 28

(ii) $n = 5$ gives $2^5 - 1 = 31$ so $16 \times 31 = 496$ is perfect.
   $496 = 1 + 2 + 4 + 8 + 16 + 31 + 62 + 124 + 248$
   $n = 7$ gives $2^7 - 1 = 127$ which is prime so $64 \times 127 = 8128$
   is perfect.

Activity 132

1 $x^2 - y^2 = (x + y)(x - y)$
   In this case $x - y = 1$ so $x^2 - y^2 = x + y$.

2 If the number being squared is n then the two other numbers being multiplied together are $n - 1$ and $n + 1$.
   Now $(n - 1)(n + 1) = n^2 - 1$
   so the product is always 1 less than n^2.

3 With powers of 3 the last digit repeats the cycle 3, 9, 7, 1.
   Powers of 2 give the sequence 2, 4, 8, 6.
   Powers of 4 give the sequence 4, 6.
   Powers of 5 and 6 just give 5 and 6.
   Powers of 7 give the sequence 7, 9, 3, 1.
   Powers of 8 give the sequence 8, 4, 2, 6.
   Powers of 9 give the sequence 9, 1.
   Note the close connection between the patterns of 3 and 7 and between those of 2 and 8.

4 The nth line consists of n consecutive odd numbers ending in the $\frac{1}{2}n(n + 1)$th odd number and their sum is equal to n^3.

5 The sum of the cubes of the first n numbers is equal to the square of the sum of the first n numbers. For example

$$1^3 + 2^3 + 3^3 + 4^3 = (1 + 2 + 3 + 4)^2$$

Activity 133

The main triads with numbers less than 50 are

3	4	5
5	12	13
7	24	25
8	15	17
9	40	41
12	35	37
20	21	29

Each give triangle area 210. (for the last two rows)

Others are also possible as multiples of these such as

6 8 10   or   15 36 39   or   16 30 34

Because of the identity

$$(m^2 - n^2)^2 + (2mn)^2 = (m^2 + n^2)^2$$

new Pythagorean triads can be easily found by giving whole number values to m and n and then calculating the numbers

$$m^2 - n^2 \quad 2mn \quad m^2 + n^2$$

Some three-dimensional examples are

2	3	6	7
1	4	8	9
3	16	24	29

Activity 134

These games have proved very stimulating and lead to some good creative mathematical thinking. They work equally well with a teacher and a class or with a small group.

Activity 135

138 × 42 = 5796	198 × 27 = 5346
483 × 12 = 5796	297 × 18 = 5346
186 × 39 = 7254	1738 × 4 = 6952
157 × 28 = 4396	1963 × 4 = 7852

Also   51 249 876 × 3 = 153 749 628
and   32 547 891 × 6 = 195 287 346

A good reference on this and many fascinating number relations is *Recreations in the Theory of Numbers* by A. H. Beiler.

Activity 136

$$1^2 + 5^2 + 6^2 \;=\; 2^2 + 3^2 + 7^2$$
$$2^2 + 4^2 + 9^2 \;=\; 1^2 + 6^2 + 8^2$$
$$3^2 + 7^2 + 8^2 \;=\; 4^2 + 5^2 + 9^2$$

Note that in each of these cases the numbers have the additional property that the equations would balance if the numbers were not squared, for example

$$1 + 5 + 6 \;=\; 2 + 3 + 7$$

Activity 137

The magic number is 40 in each case.

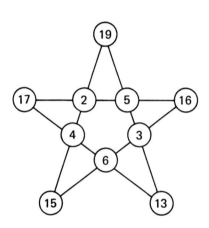

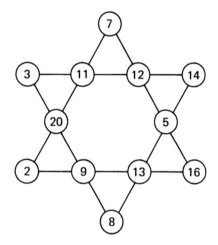

They may be solved by intelligent use of trial and error or analytically using simultaneous linear equations.

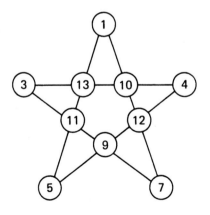

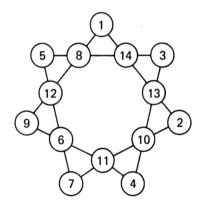

A good reference on magic stars is *Magic Squares and Cubes* by W. S. Andrews.

Activity 138

Both the puzzles here are in general circulation but if you have not met them before they offer a satisfactory challenge to your powers of reasoning. The key is to start from the left-hand end where the possible values of D (or M) are strictly limited.

(a)
```
  96233
+ 62513
-------
 158746
```

(b)
```
  9567
+ 1085
------
 10652
```

Other similar problems to try are

```
  T H R E E
+ T H R E E
    F O U R
-----------
E L E V E N
```

```
    T H I S
+      I S
   V E R Y
---------
   E A S Y
```

Activity 139

If the opponent chooses red the gambler chooses blue.
If the opponent chooses blue the gambler chooses yellow.
If the opponent chooses yellow the gambler chooses red.

In each case the gambler has a chance of winning, on average, five rolls of dice out of every nine rolls.

This is a fascinating situation. The numbers on the faces of each dice total the same and no single dice is better than both the others. To see why the blue dice is superior to the red dice consider the possible ways in which the two dice could land:

Score on red dice	Possible score on blue dice		
2	$\underline{3}$	$\underline{5}$	$\underline{7}$
4	3	$\underline{5}$	$\underline{7}$
9	3	5	$\underline{7}$

The times when blue has a larger score have been under-lined and of the nine possible combinations, each of which are equally likely, blue comes out above red on five occasions. Similarly it can be shown why yellow is superior to blue and red superior to yellow.

Activity 140

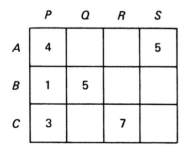

	P	Q	R	S
A	4			5
B	1	5		
C	3		7	

or

	P	Q	R	S
A		4		5
B	5	1		
C	3		7	

Both these allocations lead to a distance of 67 miles. This problem is one of a general type which has a specific method of solution although here it was expected to be done by intelligent use of trial and error.

For further reading on this type of problem read, for example, *An Introduction to Linear Programming and the Theory of Games* by S. Vajda (Methuen/Wiley) or *Mathematics in Management* by A. Battersby (Pelican).

Activity 141

The other four cards are

2	3	6	7
10	11	14	15
18	19	22	23
26	27	30	31

4	5	6	7
12	13	14	15
20	21	22	23
28	29	30	31

8	9	10	11
12	13	14	15
24	25	26	27
28	29	30	31

16	17	18	19
20	21	22	23
24	25	26	27
28	29	30	31

Based on the binary representation of number, these cards are sometimes found in Christmas crackers. What is certain is that they create much interest even when both participants know how the cards work.

Activity 142

6	1	8
7	5	3
2	9	4

(b)

9	2	10
8	7	6
4	12	5

(c)

14	3	10
5	9	13
8	15	4

(d)

11	1	12
9	8	7
4	15	5

(e)

When using the method given for generating new magic squares some care should be made in choosing the differences so that all the numbers generated are different. The method works for any numbers as the following shows.

Let a be the first number and p and q the differences. The numbers generated and the resulting magic square are

a	$a + p$	$a + 2p$
$a + q$	$a + p + q$	$a + 2p + q$
$a + 2q$	$a + p + 2q$	$a + 2p + 2q$

$a + p + 2q$	a	$a + 2p + q$
$a + 2p$	$a + p + q$	$a + 2q$
$a + q$	$a + 2p + 2q$	$a + p$

The magic number is $3(a + p + q)$ which shows that for a 3×3 magic square of whole numbers the magic number is always a multiple of 3.

Can you find a, p and q so that all the numbers in the square are prime?

Activity 143

Other sets of four numbers which total 34 in Dürer's magic square are

3	2	15	14
10	11	6	7
16	3	10	5
9	6	4	15
9	4	13	8
16	3	14	1
3	10	7	14
5	10	7	12

5	9	8	12
2	12	15	5
2	13	11	8
7	12	14	1
16	5	12	1
2	13	4	15
6	15	2	11
9	6	11	8

It is not surprising that such squares were thought to possess mystical powers.

In the Nasik magic square most of the symmetries of the Dürer square exist but in addition there are diagonal patterns such as

15	14	2	3
10	4	7	13
14	9	3	8

10	11	7	6
11	16	6	1
15	5	2	12

The fullest reference on magic squares is probably *Magic Squares and Cubes* by W. S. Andrews, but there is much of interest in *Mathematical Recreations and Essays* by W. W. Rouse Ball, and in *Amusements in Mathematics* by H. E. Dudeney.

Activity 144

The property for a 3 x 3 magic square is always true as can be proved algebraically from the general form of the square given in the commentary of Activity 142. Adding any constant number k to the numbers of a multigrade will generate a new multigrade of the same order. Suppose for example

$$A + B + C + D = a + b + c + d$$

and $\quad A^2 + B^2 + C^2 + D^2 = a^2 + b^2 + c^2 + d^2$

then $\quad (A+k) + (B+k) + (C+k) + (D+k) = A + B + C + D + 4k$
$$= a + b + c + d + 4k$$
$$= (a+k) + (b+k) + (c+k) + (d+k)$$

and $(A+k)^2 + (B+k)^2 + (C+k)^2 + (D+k)^2$
$$= A^2 + B^2 + C^2 + D^2 + 2k(A + B + C + D) + 4k^2$$
$$= a^2 + b^2 + c^2 + d^2 + 2k(a + b + c + d) + 4k^2$$
$$= (a+k)^2 + (b+k)^2 + (c+k)^2 + (d+k)^2$$

I am indebted to my colleague Donald Cross who introduced me to the idea of a multigrade and has written many articles on them.

Activity 145

The next two lines of Pascal's triangle are

$$\begin{array}{ccccccc} 1 & 6 & 15 & 20 & 15 & 6 & 1 \\ 1 & 7 & 21 & 35 & 35 & 21 & 7 & 1 \end{array}$$

Apart from the 1s at the end the other numbers are formed by adding pairs of adjacent numbers in the line above. The sum of the numbers in each row is a power of 2; the 12th line has a sum of $2^{11} = 2048$.

Powers of 11

The powers of 11 only satisfy the pattern up to 11^4. With 11^5 a carry is involved as the corresponding line in the triangle is 1, 5, 10, 10, 5, 1 and this upsets the pattern.

Hexagonal maze

1   4   6   4   1

The binomial pattern

Put $a = 1$ to see why the numbers in a row of Pascal's triangle equal a power of 2.

By putting the numbers of Pascal's triangle as a right-angled triangle pattern and working upwards it soon becomes clear that the pattern for the coefficients of $(1 + a)^{-1}$ and $(1 + a)^{-2}$ etc. also occur.

1	$^-3$	6	$^-10$	15	$^-21$	$(1 + a)^{-3}$
1	$^-2$	3	$^-4$	5	$^-6$	$(1 + a)^{-2}$
1	$^-1$	1	$^-1$	1	$^-1$	$(1 + a)^{-1}$
1	0	0	0	0	0	$(1 + a)^0$
1	1	0	0	0	0	$(1 + a)^1$
1	2	1	0	0	0	$(1 + a)^2$
1	3	3	1	0	0	$(1 + a)^3$
1	4	6	4	1	0	$(1 + a)^4$
1	5	10	10	5	1	$(1 + a)^5$

Activity 146

An interesting reference on the Fibonacci sequence is School Mathematics Project *Book 2* while *Riddles in Mathematics* by E. P. Northrop does more on the connections with nature. For a serious study a book such as *An Introduction to the Theory of Numbers* by G. H. Hardy and E. M. Wright (Oxford University Press) is recommended.

Activity 147

The rule governing the numbers in a Fibonacci sequence can be expressed as the difference equation

$$U_{n+2} = U_{n+1} + U_n$$

and its solution for the sequence starting with two 1s is

$$U_n = \frac{1}{\sqrt{5}} \left\{ \left(\frac{1 + \sqrt{5}}{2} \right)^n - \left(\frac{1 - \sqrt{5}}{2} \right)^n \right\}.$$

From the difference equation above

$$\frac{U_{n+2}}{U_{n+1}} = 1 + \frac{U_n}{U_{n+1}}$$

Now as n becomes larger U_{n+2}/U_{n+1} and U_{n+1}/U_n both approach the same limit α, so in the limit

$$\alpha = 1 + \frac{1}{\alpha}$$

giving $\alpha^2 - \alpha - 1 = 0$, from which $\alpha = \frac{1}{2}(1 + \sqrt{5})$.

To construct a regular pentagon the key is to construct a length equal to $\frac{1}{2}(1 + \sqrt{5})$. This can be done as follows.

Construct a right-angle then use your compass as a pair of dividers to mark off AB equal to 2 units and BC equal to 1 unit. Join A to C and extend.

By Pythagoras' theorem $AC = \sqrt{5}$ units. Use the compass to mark off D 1 unit from C, then AD is $1 + \sqrt{5}$ and it only remains to bisect AD to get a length of $\frac{1}{2}(1 + \sqrt{5})$. These should be straightforward!

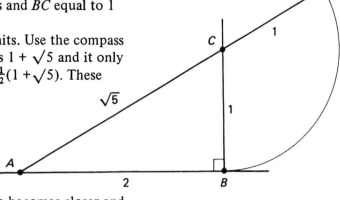

With the new sequence given the ratio becomes closer and closer to 2.

Another interesting way of generating the Fibonacci sequence is to consider the effect of successive powers of the

matrix $\begin{pmatrix} 0 & 1 \\ 1 & 1 \end{pmatrix}$ on a number pair such as $\begin{pmatrix} 1 \\ 1 \end{pmatrix}$

$$\begin{pmatrix} 0 & 1 \\ 1 & 1 \end{pmatrix} \begin{pmatrix} 1 \\ 1 \end{pmatrix} = \begin{pmatrix} 1 \\ 2 \end{pmatrix}, \quad \begin{pmatrix} 0 & 1 \\ 1 & 1 \end{pmatrix}^2 \begin{pmatrix} 1 \\ 1 \end{pmatrix} = \begin{pmatrix} 2 \\ 3 \end{pmatrix}, \quad \begin{pmatrix} 0 & 1 \\ 1 & 1 \end{pmatrix}^3 \begin{pmatrix} 1 \\ 1 \end{pmatrix} = \begin{pmatrix} 3 \\ 5 \end{pmatrix}$$

and so on. If the ordered pairs are plotted as vectors then their gradient approaches the golden section ratio.

Further references on the Fibonacci sequence and golden section ratio abound. Try *Mathematical Snapshots* by H. Steinhaus or *Symmetry* by Weyl or *Pattern and Design with Dynamic Symmetry* by Edward B. Edwards.

Activity 148

The weights are 1 kg, 3 kg, 9 kg and 27 kg. By putting the weights on either scale pan then all the weights from 1 to 40 can be achieved. For example

$$11 = 9 + 3 - 1 \qquad 20 = 27 + 3 - 9 - 1$$

Activity 149

The lengths must be in the ratio of $\sqrt{2} : 1$ as

$$\frac{x}{1} = \frac{1}{x/2}$$

giving $\qquad x^2 = 2$

from which $\qquad x = \sqrt{2}$

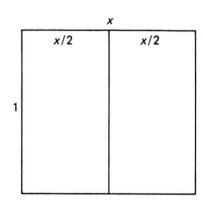

Activity 150

Middle layer

23	3	16
7	14	21
12	25	5

Bottom layer

18	22	2
20	9	13
4	11	27

For much more on magic cubes see *Magic Squares and Cubes* by W. S. Andrews.

Activity 151

Compare 9 balls with 9 balls and leave 9 in the box. If the scales balance then the heavy ball is in the box, if not then the 9 balls which go down contains the heavy ball. Either way, after one balance the faulty ball has been narrowed down to a set of 9. Divide this set of 9 into three sets of 3 After this you will have narrowed down the faulty ball to 3 and one more balance sorts it out.

A similar but much harder problem is to find the odd ball from 13 in three balances if all you know is that the odd ball has a different weight to the other 12.

Activity 152

(i) Do the division, subtract the whole number part of the quotient, and multiply the resulting decimal number by 729.

One calculator gave

$$89\ 328 \div 729 = 122.534\ 97$$

$$0.534\ 97 \times 729 = 389.993\ 13$$

Because of the limitations in the capacity of a calculator there are errors in the last few digits but the remainder can be confidently given as the nearest whole number, 390.

Check by seeing that $(729 \times 122) + 390 = 89\ 328$

Alternatively from the initial division the remainder can be found as

$$89\ 328 - (729 \times 122) = 390$$

thus avoiding the need to round off.

(ii) As $\alpha^3 = 200$ can be written as

$$\alpha^2 = \frac{200}{\alpha}$$

from which $\alpha = \sqrt{\left(\dfrac{200}{\alpha}\right)}$

it follows that if x is an approximation to the cube root of 200 then $\sqrt{(200/x)}$ is a better approximation. For example if $x_1 = 6$ is taken as the first approximation to $\sqrt[3]{200}$ then take

$$x_2 = \sqrt{\frac{200}{6}} \doteqdot 5.7735$$

$$x_3 = \sqrt{\frac{200}{5.7735}} \doteqdot 5.885\ 66$$

$$x_4 = \sqrt{\frac{200}{5.885\ 66}} \doteqdot 5.829\ 31$$

$$x_5 = \sqrt{\frac{200}{5.829\ 31}} \doteqdot 5.857\ 42 \text{ etc.}$$

This method converges automatically to the required number. It may not be as quick as a skilled operator using trial and error but it would be easy to program.

(iii) What is infinity on your calculator!

Start with a string of 9s and then keep reducing until you get other than 0 for an answer.

Activity 153

This magic hexagon was first discovered by an Englishman, T. Vickers, who published it in the December 1958 *Mathematical Gazette*.

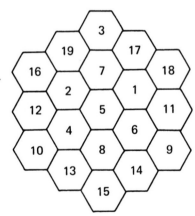

Activity 154

The game of Nim is analysed in *Mathematical Recreations and Essays* by W. W. Rouse Ball and there is an interesting chapter in *We Built our Own Computers* by A. B. Bolt describing a machine which could play the game.

The game is interesting because every position of the game can be classified as 'safe' or 'unsafe'.

From a safe position a player can only create an unsafe position no matter how many counters he moves. However from an unsafe position it is possible to move to either a safe or an unsafe position. Thus a player who has analysed the game can always move from an unsafe position to a safe position and beat his opponent.

There are many more unsafe positions than safe positions but to proceed it is necessary to find out how to decide which are which.

Take the example given in the description of the game. First convert the number of counters in each heap into binary and add up the digits in each column without resorting to carry.

	Binary form
7	111
9	1001
6	110
Digit sum	1222

For a safe position the digit sum for each column must be an even number. Hence the position here is unsafe.

To move to a safe position the second heap could be reduced to 1

then 7	111	is a safe position
1	1	
6	110	
	222	

Why is this the only safe move from this position? Other safe positions are, for example, (2, 4, 6) (2, 5, 7) (1, 2, 3) (7, 10, 13).

Playing against an uninitiated player a player who can use the strategy described here should win nine times out of ten but he cannot win if the starting position is unsafe and his opponent moves to a safe move from it and on every subsequent move. Faced with a safe position the best strategy is to remove just one counter (i.e. do as little as possible) in the hope that your opponent's next move will be to an unsafe position.

FURTHER RESOURCES

Books

The books in this list do not require a high level of mathematical training to be understood although many of the concepts presented in them are at the heart of mathematics.

W. S. Andrews, *Magic Squares and Cubes* (Dover)

B. Averbach and O. Chein, *Mathematics: Problem Solving Through Recreational Mathematics* (W. H. Freeman)

D. St. P. Barnard, *Figure it Out* (Pan)

Stephen Barr, *Experiments in Topology* (John Murray)

David Bergamini, *Mathematics* (Life Science Library)

A. H. Beiler, *Recreations in the Theory of Numbers* (Dover)

Pierre Berloquin, *Geometric Games* (Unwin Paperbacks)

A. B. Bolt, *We Built Our Own Computers* (Cambridge University Press)

A. B. Bolt and J. E. Hiscocks, *Machines, Mechanisms and Mathematics* (Chatto and Windus for the Schools Council Mathematics for the Majority Project)

Edward de Bono, *The Five-Day Course in Thinking* (Pelican)

R. Courant and H. Robbins, *What is Mathematics?* (Oxford University Press)

H. M. Cundy and A. P. Rollett, *Mathematical Models* (Oxford University Press)

H. E. Dudeney, *Amusements in Mathematics* (Dover)

H. E. Dudeney, *The Canterbury Puzzles* (Dover)

H. E. Dudeney, *Puzzles and Curious Problems* (Fontana)

Edward B. Edwards, *Pattern and Design with Dynamic Symmetry* (Dover)

The Graphic Work of M. C. Escher (Pan)

Aaron, J. Friedland, *Puzzles in Mathematics and Logic* (Dover)

G. Gamow and M. Stern, *Puzzle-math* (Macmillan)

Martin Gardner, *Mathematical Puzzles and Diversions* (Pelican)

Martin Gardner, *More Mathematical Puzzles and Diversions* (Pelican)

Martin Gardner, *Further Mathematical Diversions* (Pelican)

Martin Gardner, *Mathematical Carnival* (Pelican)

Martin Gardner, *Mathematics, Magic and Mystery* (Pelican)

Martin Gardner, *New Mathematical Diversions* (Allen and Unwin)

Solomon W. Golomb, *Polyominoes* (Allen and Unwin)

L. A. Graham, *Ingenious Mathematical Problems and Methods* (Dover)

Gerald Jenkins and Anne Wild, *Make Shapes, Series no 1, no 2 and no 3* (Tarquin Publications)

S. I. Jones, *Mathematical Wrinkles* (Norwood Press – likely to be unobtainable)

E. Kasner and J. Newman, *Mathematics and the Imagination* (Bell)

E. H. Lockwood, *A Book of Curves* (Cambridge University Press)

E. P. Northrop, *Riddles in Mathematics* (Pelican)

H. Phillips, *My Best Puzzles in Mathematics* (Dover)

W. W. Rouse Ball, *Mathematical Recreations and Essays* (Macmillan)

Royal Vale Heath, *Mathemagic* (Dover)

Dale Seymour, *Sum Puzzles* (Creative Publications, Inc.)

H. Steinhaus, *Mathematical Snapshots* (Oxford University Press)

H. Steinhaus, *One Hundred Problems in Elementary Mathematics* (Pergamon)

Frank Tapson, *Take Two! 32 board games for 2 players* (A. and C. Black Ltd)

Frank Tapson and Alan Parr, *Pick a Pair! 30 board games for 2 players* (A. and C. Black Ltd)

P. Van Delft and J. Botermans, *Creative Puzzles of the World* (Cassell)

A. F. Wells, *The Third Dimension in Chemistry* (Oxford University Press)

Magazines

Mathematical Pie, published termly, available from West View, Fiveways, Warwick

Mathematics in School, published five times a year, available from the subscriptions manager, Longman Group Ltd, Directories and Periodicals Division, 43/45 Annandale Street, Edinburgh EH7 4AT

Mathematics Teaching, published quarterly, available from the Association of Teachers of Mathematics, Market Street Chambers, Nelson, Lancashire BB9 7LN

Games

Amoeba (Louis Marx)
Backgammon
Black Box (Waddingtons)
Blockbuster (D. Cross, School of Education, Exeter University)
Check Lines (Tri–ang)
Chess
Cluedo (Waddingtons)
Connect 4 (Milton Bradley)
Dominoes
Draughts
Four Sight (Invicta)
Go
Hexagonal Chess
Interaction (Waddingtons)
L–Game (de Bono)
Magic Cube (Pentangle)
Mancala (Spear's Games)
Master Mind (Invicta)
Monopoly (Waddingtons)
Nine Men's Morris
Noughts and Crosses in three dimensions (various commercial
    forms, e.g. Fours and Space Lines)
Othello (Peter Pan Playthings)
Reversi (Spear's Games)
Skirrid (Eliot–Taylor)
Solitaire
Spirograph (Denys Fisher)
Touch Down (Invicta – formerly marketed as Pressups)
Trap (Ideal)

Some useful sources of games and puzzles are:

Games Centre, 16 Hanway Street, London W1A 2LS
Pentangle, Over Wallop, Hants SO2O 8NT
Double Games Ltd, 10 Hampstead Gardens, London NW11